THE PICTURE DICTIONARY
FOR CHILDREN

by Garnette Watters *and* S. A. Courtis

Prepared by two of America's most famous educators of the learning-to-read child, THE PICTURE DICTIONARY FOR CHILDREN has many features not found in any other children's dictionary. One of the most important of these is the fact that this is the *only* child's dictionary which shows words both in type and in *handwriting*. Thus, from the very beginning, the young reader is made familiar with each word in both its printed and script forms.

Moreover, the 5084 words and the 1450 pictures in THE PICTURE DICTION-ARY FOR CHILDREN make it the most complete dictionary for the beginning reader.

This is a book your child will be proud to own. It will be his "very own" dictionary, a book in which he can browse over and over again, learning new words with the help of the simple and attractive pictures alongside. Without any conscious effort on his part, he will have acquired the "dictionary habit," a habit which will lead in later life to the power over words so essential to success.

And, equally important, THE PICTURE DICTIONARY FOR CHILDREN is a book which will give him many hours of sheer enjoyment. Your child will echo the words of the millions of children who have used the earlier editions of this book:

"This dictionary is fun!"

A FIRST GUIDE TO THE MEANINGS,
SPELLINGS, AND USES OF WORDS
AND A FASCINATING INTRODUCTION
TO THE ADVENTURE OF BUILDING
A VOCABULARY.

THE
PICTURE
DICTIONARY
FOR CHILDREN

BY GARNETTE WATTERS
FORMERLY DIRECTOR OF THE LANGUAGE DEPARTMENT OF THE PUBLIC SCHOOLS,
HAMTRAMCK, MICHIGAN
AND
STUART A. COURTIS
PROFESSOR OF EDUCATION, EMERITUS, UNIVERSITY OF MICHIGAN

PICTURES BY
DORIS AND MARION HENDERSON
AND BARRY BART

PUBLISHERS · GROSSET & DUNLAP · NEW YORK

A FILMWAYS COMPANY

1977 Printing
Library of Congress Catalog Card Number: 76-53875
ISBN: 0-448-14002-0 (Paperback Edition)
ISBN: 0-448-03523-5 (Library Edition)
Copyright 1939, 1945, 1948, 1958, 1968, 1972, by Western Publishing Company, Inc.
Designed and produced by Western Publishing Company, Inc.
Printed in the United States of America

Dear Boys and Girls:

In this book we have hidden many words. They are like gold, for they will help you when you need them. You will want them for your word friends. Hunt for them.

> They will help you to read;
> They will help you to spell;
> They will help you to write
> And to say things well.

You will have fun hunting for new words.

You will like the pictures.

You will enjoy reading the stories.

You will enjoy finding, all by yourself, words that will help you to read, to write, and to spell.

We hope you will like this "Picture Dictionary" we have made for you.

The Authors

How to Find Words in This Book

1. Look at the first letter in the word you want to find.

2. Put your right thumb on the A at the side of this page and the rest of your fingers at the back of the book.

3. Move your thumb down the page. Stop when you find the letter that is just like the first letter in your word.

4. Keep your right thumb on the letter.

5. Let the pages fly past your thumb until you find the letter you are looking for. It will be the letter in the white circle.

6. Move your fingers down the pages until you find the word you are looking for.

7. Look at the picture if there is one.

8. Read what the words say.

9. Sometimes the words are in a box, like this:

Mother said it was | **bedtime.**
time to go to bed.

10. If you cannot find the word you are looking for at the side, find the word that looks nearly like your word. Then find the words opposite it that have these marks around them ( ) . These words will help you build big words from little words.

11. If you want to learn to write the word, try to copy it like the written word.

EXPLANATION OF
THE PICTURE DICTIONARY FOR CHILDREN

A dictionary is an indispensable element in the equipment of every educated adult, but it is a formidable and discouraging obstacle to beginning readers. Yet the needs of the children in the early grades for the assistance a dictionary renders in language activities are as real and as pressing as those of their parents. It is surprising that the world has had to wait until the twentieth century for a dictionary written to meet the needs of little children.

THE PICTURE DICTIONARY is less and more than a children's dictionary: less, in that the pronunciation, derivations, and much of the other intricate machinery that constitute the dictionary of the adult is unsuited to the immaturity of beginning readers, and has been omitted; more, in that special care has been taken to present words by pictures, comparisons, context, print, and script in ways that make it possible for very, very young readers to find meanings for unfamiliar symbols, to discover new words related in meaning and spelling to known words, and to adventure on their own initiative in all the activities of language comprised in the conventional school subjects of reading, writing, and spelling.

This is a child's own book. The words have been selected with children's needs in mind, and the illustrations, type, and arrangement have been adjusted to childish levels of development. Every detail of preparation has been planned for the purpose of *helping* little children who use this book. Here is a children's text which is not designed to be "taught" but "used," and whose use will automatically contribute to worthwhile growth.

Progressive teachers into whose hands this volume falls will welcome a new instrument for developing self-direction, self-appraisal, and self-control in children. The average teacher who gives it a trial with her classes will quickly be convinced of its value. Traditionally-minded teachers will find little difficulty in fitting the book into the conventional scheme of memorization and drill. Fortunately, today, all of us are coming to recognize more and more that true growth arises only from self-directed purposeful activity, and that for real learning a child must teach himself. Purpose proves to be the key to educational efficiency, and the intelligent teacher will make plain to the children the potentialities for self-help which the volume offers, practice them in the techniques of its use, and then leave the rest to the children and the book. Any child in the first or second grade who has the desire to read a story, who knows "how" to use this PICTURE DICTIONARY, and who has the will to put his knowledge to practical use, can study out by himself the meanings in most books up to a high third-grade level. In spelling and language work the book is no less effective. By its help all language activities may be transformed from formal, subject-matter, teacher-directed *acquisitions* into natural lifelike *activities*, productive of growth in personality and power.

In selecting the words for this PICTURE DICTIONARY, it was necessary to determine the range of words required to serve adequately the needs and purposes of children in the primary grades. Words were gathered from written work, oral conversation, and an analysis of forty-six readers for the primary grades.

A WORD TO TEACHERS

A book may be used in a great variety of ways, each appropriate for a different purpose, but the *most effective* way to use it is in accordance with the purpose which prompted its formulation. The Picture Dictionary may be used as any ordinary textbook is used by teachers who are interested in teaching reading, writing, spelling, and similar language skills. Children will enjoy looking at the pictures, reading the short stories about the words they know, puzzling out the meanings of words they do not know, learning the alphabet, and so on. However, the book was designed specifically for use by those teachers who believe that educational development is best achieved when it occurs spontaneously and incidentally as a by-product of self-directed, purposeful activity.

For the guidance of teachers who are in the process of shifting from traditional to progressive methods, the following suggestions are offered:

1. **AIM** • In using this Picture Dictionary let your goal be "**to help children to help themselves.**" Do nothing for them that they can be stimulated to do for themselves. Remember that each individual is different from every other individual and has the right to follow his own best path of development, choosing in terms of his own taste, growing at his own rate and by his own choice of method.

Let your responsibility be presenting situations, stimulating purposes, helping children plan, act, judge, generalize, conserve, and appraise the results of their purposing. Have no fear if the children fail to learn to read, to spell, etc., as rapidly as you had anticipated. Mastery of these skills will result from purposeful activity. Eventually each child will acquire ability mature enough to deal successfully with situations which involve the use of the language arts, but his growth as a person, his integrity as an individual, demand that he shall have freedom to develop in terms of his own nature.

2. MEANS • The Picture Dictionary is **a tool;** it should always be used as **a means to an end,** never as an end in itself. The teacher should create situations in which need is apparent to the child before putting the means of satisfying that need in his hands. Always have in mind a purpose beyond the means which will predetermine the use of the means itself. The child must have the desire to achieve some purpose and must have met some obstacle to the achievement of that goal that the Picture Dictionary can help remove, **before** he is given the book itself. For instance, if a child finds a story about a dog in his reader and really desires to enjoy the story but comes upon words like "excited," or "rushed," the meaning of which he does not know, his enjoyment of the story is blocked. The teacher might say, "Here is a book that will help you. I can show you how to find words you do not know in this book. It will tell you what the words mean. When you know how to use this Picture Dictionary you can read any story." The child will appreciate that the dictionary is a tool which he can use to help him achieve his own purpose of enjoying printed stories.

3. PREREQUISITES • The Picture Dictionary is a supplementary book. As soon as beginning readers have grasped the concept of words as symbols for experiences and ideas, the use of the dictionary may be begun. Its use should continue until the maturity of the reader has led him into vocabularies beyond the nearly five thousand words in the Picture Dictionary (about third grade development). By this time he will be ready to change from the simple Picture Dictionary to some more advanced dictionary for children.

4. USES • As soon as little first graders have learned to recognize any words as symbols for objects, they will enjoy searching through the Picture Dictionary for words that they can identify by the pictures. This is probably the simplest use of the Picture Dictionary.

The next step is more difficult but equally enjoyable: searching through the Picture Dictionary for the names of objects. The teacher puts on the board a series of drawings—a cat, a dog, a cow—and, the child who first finds the corresponding picture and name in his book comes and prints the name of the object on the board, copying it from his dictionary. This game gives the child a sense of delightful power. The next step is easy. The teacher prints unknown words like "rabbit" or "tree" on the board and the child looks them up to discover their meanings from their pictures. This of course is the true use of the dictionary.

A child does not need **to know** his alphabet to look up words; he has to be able only to match letters, and with very immature beginning readers this matching activity can well be carried on as a game. Note that although a child may not know the alphabet when he first begins to use the dictionary, he soon learns it through continual use. When the children become fairly free in using the alphabet, there comes a time when the slower children will profit by drills designed to give the child systematic and conscious control over the alphabet as such. It is better to let the children **grow** into a knowledge of the alphabet **before** drill than to attempt to teach the alphabet specifically first. The same thing is true of phonics. Help the child **generalize** the sounds of the letters from his experiences with words rather than try to teach him the sounds as an aid to reading words.

Before very long first graders will begin of themselves to enjoy reading the short stories (definitions) under the pictures in the Dictionary, an activity which should be encouraged. The Picture Dictionary is essentially a series of stimuli and as soon as this activity makes its appearance, it should be highly praised and rejoiced over. Once a child gets the idea that self-help is possible, he will use his dictionary to tackle any reading. Indeed the danger is that he will expect too much of his tool.

It is only a **first** dictionary and is most valuable to readers on the levels found in the first three grades. When a child first finds a word in his reading that is not presented in the Picture Dictionary, it will be necessary for the teacher to tell him what the word means, but as soon as the demands on the teacher begin to multiply, it is time to introduce the children to a dictionary on a higher level. The transition should be gradual, occurring more and more frequently, until at last the child himself abandons the Picture Dictionary for a more advanced one.

A teacher will do well to have two kinds of learning experiences in her class. At first the children will spend most of their time in formal reading exercises directed by the teacher, with occasional games in the use of the Picture Dictionary to break the monotony and to serve the purposes of review and stimulation. Then, as some children progress faster than others, they can be set free for self-directed reading involving self-help use of the dictionary. The teacher's group will gradually become smaller and smaller so that she can focus her attention on the more difficult cases. From time to time the whole class will be brought together for testing and review, but for the most part the Picture Dictionary makes it possible for a teacher soon to **individualize completely** her work and let each child progress at his own rate, and read in terms of his own tastes.

A wise teacher will grade her books and supplementary reading materials and see that each child reads material at his own reading level. If a child must look up **every** word in the Picture Dictionary he gets little pleasure from his activity, but if he knows most of the words in a book, it is a pleasure to master those he does not know. By arranging a carefully graded series of readers, a teacher can insure both continuous progress on the part of the child and continuous enjoyment of his reading.

5. **USES OTHER THAN READING** • The use of the Picture Dictionary should not be restricted to the reading class. In his English work, if a child is in doubt about the spelling of a word, he should be encouraged to look it up in his dictionary. Similarly, the dictionary furnishes script models for the writing class. A child meets unknown words in arithmetic and other

classes and the use of the dictionary should be encouraged in these classes also. In other words the wise teacher takes care to develop the "dictionary habit" from the very first grade.

6. **APPRAISAL** • The Picture Dictionary may be used for testing purposes in reading, writing, spelling, etc. Sentences involving new words may be put on the board and the whole class tested as to the rate at which the children are able to read and write their interpretations. Words which they are able to recognize may be classified and written in alphabetical lists. There is scarcely any phase of the language arts for which the ingenious and resourceful teacher cannot use the Picture Dictionary as a test booklet.

By far the most significant appraisal, however, is the child's own spontaneous use of the Picture Dictionary for his own purposes. The child who of his own volition takes out the dictionary and pores over its pages, reading and rereading the words and stories he knows, puzzling out ever more of those he does not know, is making satisfactory progress and learning to love to read. The child who insists on having his dictionary handy whenever he tries to read and who is adventurous and courageous in tackling by means of his dictionary any printed matter to which he has access has acquired ideas and powers far more valuable than any mere reading skill. It is to be hoped that all teachers into whose hands the Picture Dictionary comes will capitalize its many opportunities for the development of self-direction, self-appraisal, and self-control as well as those for the development of the narrower language purposes and skills.

John has **a** dog. I saw **a** bird.	**a** *a*
Baby is **able** to walk alone. She can walk alone.	**able** a-ble *able*
Bob told a story **about** a dog. It is about three o'clock. around	**about** a-bout *about*
The picture is above the table. over	**above** a-bove *above*
The car ran into a post. It was an **accident.** (accidents)	**accident** ac-ci-dent *accident*
The baby is sick. His stomach **aches.** It pains him all the time. (ache ached aching)	**aches** *aches*
This is an **acorn.** It is the seed of an oak tree. (acorns)	**acorn** a-corn *acorn*
Bob threw the ball across the room. to the other side of	**across** a-cross *across*

A
B
C
D
E
F
G
H
I
J
K
L
M
N
O
P
Q
R
S
T
U
V
W
X
Y
Z

B
C
D
E
F
G
H
I
J
K
L
M
N
O
P
Q
R
S
T
U
V
W
X
Y
Z

act *act*	Mother told the children to |**act**| well. do Running, singing, and all the things you do are **acts**. (acts acted acting)
add *add*	If you |**add**| 2 apples and 2 put together more apples, you have 4 apples. This sign + means to **add** or put together. (adds adding added)
admire ad-mire *admire*	Do you |**ad mire**| good stories? like (admires admired admiring)
advice ad-vice *advice*	I made a kite. Father gave me some good |**advice.** suggestions.|
afraid a-fraid *afraid*	The cat is |**afraid**| of the dog. scared
Africa Af-ri-ca *Africa*	**Africa** is a land across the sea. Many people live in **Africa**.

Bob went to bed right **after** supper. The cat ran **after** the mouse.	**after** af-ter *after*
We eat lunch at 12 o'clock noon. After 12 o'clock noon, it is **afternoon.** (afternoons)	**afternoon** af-ter-noon *afternoon*
We work first. We play **afterwards.** at a later time.	**afterwards** af-ter-wards *afterwards*
The girl jumped the rope **again** another time and **again.** another time.	**again** a-gain *again*
The ladder leans **against** the wall. It touches the wall. Our team played **against** yours and we won.	**against** a-gainst *against*
What is your **age?** How many years old are you?	**age** *age*
Father went to work a long time **ago.**	**ago** a-go *ago*

agree
a-gree
agree

The boys do not **agree.**
think alike.

(agrees   agreed   agreeing)

ahead
a-head
ahead

The girl is **ahead**
in front
of the boy.

aim
aim

We **aim** to do our best.
try

The boy **aimed** the arrow
pointed
at the tree.

(aims   aimed   aiming)

air
air

Father is putting **air**
in the tire.

Bob put up the window.
Fresh **air** blew in.

airplane
air-plane
airplane

This is an **airplane.**
(airplanes)

airport
air-port
airport

This is an **airport.**
Airplanes take off
from an **airport**
and land there.

(airports)

The door stood **ajar.**		**ajar**
It was open slightly.		a-jar
(a-jar)		*ajar*

An alarm clock   A fire alarm box

When the fire **alarm** sounds,
   the firemen go to put out the fire.
    (alarms   alarmed   alarming)

alarm
a-larm
alarm

These houses are | **alike.**
the same. |

alike
a-like
alike

The auto hit the chicken,
   but the chicken is still **alive.**

It is not dead.

alive
a-live
alive

"Someone has been eating my porridge, too,

   and she ate it | **all** | up,"
    | every bit |

said the wee little bear.

all
all

This is an **alligator.**

Alligators live in water.
   (alligators)

alligator
al-li-ga-tor
alligator

Mother will not | **allow** me to | go.
    | let me |

   (allows   allowed   allowing)

allow
al-low
allow

B
C
D
E
F
G
H
I
J
K
L
M
N
O
P
Q
R
S
T
U
V
W
X
Y
Z

almost
al-most
almost

It is almost time to go home.
nearly

alone
a-lone
alone

Baby stands alone.
all by herself.

Mary goes to school alone.

No one goes with her.

along
a-long
along

We walked along the road.

Mary went to school, and Bob went along, too.

already
al-read-y
already

The boys have come already.
by this time.

also
al-so
also

John has a ball.

I have a ball also.
too.

always
al-ways
always

Bob is always good to his dog.
at all times

Mary always reads first.

Every time she reads first.

am
am

He put in his thumb

And pulled out a plum

And said, "What a good boy am I!"

I am a good boy, too.

The land we live in is called **America.**		**America** A-mer-i-ca *America*
I live in America. I am an **American.** This is an **American** flag. (Americans)		**American** A-mer-i-can *American*
Grass grows **among** the flowers. Bob divided the cake **among** three boys.		**among** a-mong *among*
I have **an** apple. I have **an** orange.		**an** *an*
This castle is ancient. very old.		**ancient** an-cient *ancient*
We dance **and** sing, "Jack **and** Jill went up the hill."		**and** *and*
I wanted to go to the picnic. Father would not let me go. This made me **angry.** (angrier angriest anger)		**angry** an-gry *angry*

21

A B C D E F G H I J K L M N O P Q R S T U V W X Y Z

B
C
D
E
F
G
H
I
J
K
L
M
N
O
P
Q
R
S
T
U
V
W
X
Y
Z

animal
an-i-mal
animal

A pony is an **animal**.

Two cows are two **animals**.

(animals)

announcer
an-nounc-er
announcer

The **announcer** tells

who will sing on the program.

(announce announces announced announcing)

another
an-oth-er
another

This is one car.　　This is **another** car.

answer
an-swer
answer

Mother called to Bob but he did not **answer**.

Our teacher asked a question.

Mary knew the **answer**.

(answers　answered　answering)

ant
ant

An **ant** is an insect.

(ants)

any
an-y
any

Baa, baa, black sheep,

Have you **any** wool?
some

anybody
an-y-bod-y
anybody

I heard the doorbell ring.

I did not see **anybody**.
a person.

I did not see **anyone** coming. a person	**anyone** an-y-one *anyone*
We heard an airplane in the sky, but we could not see **anything.**	**anything** an-y-thing *anything*

Mary cannot go to the party,
    but I will go **anyway.**
    nevertheless.
	anyway
	 an-y-way
	 anyway

Sit **anywhere** you like. in any place	**anywhere** an-y-where *anywhere*
The man took the radio **apart.** to pieces. Mary stood **apart** away from the other children.	**apart** a-part *apart*
An **ape** is a kind of monkey. He has no tail like some monkeys. (apes)	**ape** *ape*
Soon the stars will **appear** in the sky. come out (appears appeared appearing)	**appear** ap-pear *appear*
This is an **apple.** **Apples** are good to eat. (apples)	**apple** ap-ple *apple*

April A-pril *April*	**April** showers bring May flowers. **April** is the fourth month of the year.
apron a-pron *apron*	This is my mother's **apron.** (aprons)
aquarium a-quar-i-um *aquarium*	The fish are in an **aquarium.** a bowl of water. (aquariums)
arbor ar-bor *arbor*	Grapevines climb on an **arbor.** a frame. (arbors)
are *are*	The boys **are** running. The girls **are** running. The children **are** running.
aren't *aren't*	The children **aren't** at home. are not
arm *arm*	The man is holding out his **arm.** (arms)
armchair arm-chair *armchair*	This chair is an **armchair.** It has arms on the sides. (armchairs)
army ar-my *army*	There are many soldiers in the **army.** (armies)

The dog is running **around** the tree.

The train goes **around** and **around** on the track.

around
a-round
around

I **arrive** home early every day.
reach

(arrives   arrived   arriving)

arrive
ar-rive
arrive

This is an **arrow**.

Bob has a bow and **arrow.**
(arrows)

arrow
ar-row
arrow

John draws pictures in **art** classes.

Sewing, like music, is an **art.**
(arts)

art
art

The boy is not **as** big **as** the girl.

as
as

Sometimes children act badly.

Afterwards they feel **ashamed.**

ashamed
a-shamed
ashamed

Bob pushed the table **aside.**
to one side.

aside
a-side
aside

Can you go with me?

I will **ask** my mother.
(asks   asked   asking)

ask
ask

A
B
C
D
E
F
G
H
I
J
K
L
M
N
O
P
Q
R
S
T
U
V
W
X
Y
Z

asleep a-sleep *asleep*	Baby has gone to bed. She is sound **asleep.**
astronaut as-tro-naut *astronaut*	The **astronaut** is flying his spaceship through space. (astronauts)
at *at*	Where is Baby? Baby is **at** the table. We will come **at** five o'clock.
ate *ate*	Baby **ate** her bread and milk. (eat eats eating)
atom at-om *atom*	All things are made of tiny parts. Each part is called an **atom.** We cannot see **atoms.** (atoms)
attention at-ten-tion *attention*	Mother called the children. They were playing. They did not pay any **attention** to her.
August Au-gust *August*	**August** is the eighth month of the year.
aunt *aunt*	My father's sister is my **aunt.** My mother's sister is my **aunt,** too. (aunts)

We ride in our **automobile.**
(automobiles)

automobile
au-to-mo-bile
automobile

Leaves come out on the trees in the spring.
Leaves fall off the trees in the **autumn.**

autumn
au-tumn
autumn

This man is an **aviator.**
He flies an airplane.
(aviators)

aviator
a-vi-a-tor
aviator

Baby is **awake.**
She is not sleeping.
(awakes   awakened   awakening   awoke)

awake
a-wake
awake

Bob rode **away** on his bicycle.
Baby walked **away**
from the window.

away
a-way
away

This is an **ax.**
This man is cutting down the tree
with an **ax.**
(axes)

ax
ax

baby
ba-by
baby

Our **baby** cannot walk yet.
(babies)

back
back

The boy is riding on the horse's **back.**

The boy sits **back of** the girl.
behind

See Father **back** the car
out of the garage.

Mother has gone, but she will be **back** soon.

Bob sits in the **back** of the room.
(backs   backed   backing)

bacon
ba-con
bacon

This meat is **bacon.**

I like **bacon** and eggs.

bad
bad

Bob is a good boy.
not a **bad**

bag
bag

We carry things in **bags.**

A handbag   A paper bag
(bags)

baggage
bag-gage
baggage

The porter
puts the **baggage** on the train.
trunks and bags

28

Mother made a cake.

She put it in the oven to | **bake.**
cook. |

(bakes   baked   baking)

bake
bake

A **baker** makes bread and cake to sell.
(bakers)

baker
bak-er
baker

These boxes | **balance.**
weigh the same. |

(balances   balanced   balancing)

balance
bal-ance
balance

This is a | **bale** | of cotton.
big bundle |

(bales)

bale
bale

Children like to play with a **ball.**
(balls)

ball
ball

Mary has a **balloon.**
She bought the **balloon** in a store.
Most **balloons** are round.

(balloons)

balloon
bal-loon
balloon

One banana   A bunch of bananas
(bananas)

banana
ba-nan-a
banana

A
B
C
D
E
F
G
H
I
J
K
L
M
N
O
P
Q
R
S
T
U
V
W
X
Y
Z

A
B
C
D
E
F
G
H
I
J
K
L
M
N
O
P
Q
R
S
T
U
V
W
X
Y
Z

band
band

This is our **band.**
We play music to march by.
(bands)

bang
bang

Bob shut the door with a loud **bang.** noise.

(bangs   banged   banging)

bank
bank

A toy bank   A city bank
We put money in a **bank.**

The dock is on the **bank** shore

of the river.
(banks)

bar
bar

This is a **bar** of soap.

This window has **bars.**

(bars)

barber
bar-ber
barber

The **barber** cuts Bobby's hair.

(barbers)

bare
bare

The cupboard was **bare.**
This hand has a glove on it.
This hand is **bare.**

barks
barks

The dog **barks** at the cat.
(bark   barked   barking)

30

The farmer put the horse in the **barn**. He keeps hay in the **barn,** too. (barns)	**barn** *barn*
The barn stands in the **barnyard**. (barnyards)	**barnyard** barn-yard *barnyard*
This is a **barrel**. We put apples in **barrels**. (barrels)	**barrel** bar-rel *barrel*
The boys like to play **baseball**. They bat the ball and run around the bases. They play this game with a **baseball**. (baseballs)	**baseball** base-ball *baseball*
This is a **basket** filled with apples. (baskets)	**basket** bas-ket *basket*
This is a baseball **bat**. We **bat** / hit the ball with the **bat**. (bats batted batting)	**bat** *bat*
This is a **bat**. It looks like a mouse with wings. (bats)	**bat** *bat*
Baby is having a **bath**. (baths)	**bath** *bath*

31

A
B
C
D
E
F
G
H
I
J
K
L
M
N
O
P
Q
R
S
T
U
V
W
X
Y
Z

bathroom
bath-room
bathroom

This is a **bathroom.**

It is the room
in which we bathe.

(bathrooms)

bathtub
bath-tub
bathtub

Here is a **bathtub.**
(bathtubs)

bay
bay

A **bay** is part of the sea.

It is a big body of water.

Boats sail on the **bay.**
(bays)

be
be

Jack said, "I will **be** a good boy."
(being   been)

beach
beach

We like to play in the sand
on the **beach.**
(beaches)

beads
beads

This is a string of **beads.**
(bead)

beans
beans

These are **beans.**

Beans are good to eat.
(bean)

bear
bear

This is a **bear.**

Bears are white, brown, or black.
(bears)

This man has a **beard** on his chin.

This man does not have a **beard** on his chin.

(beards)

beard
beard

A **beast** is an animal.

A lion is a **beast.**

(beasts)

beast
beast

Did you ever **beat** a drum?

Mother **beats** the eggs with the egg beater.

The bad boy | **beats** | his dog.
            | whips |

(beats   beating   beaten)

beat
beat

The flowers are | **beautiful.** |
                | pretty. |

beautiful
beau-ti-ful
beautiful

This animal is a **beaver.**

He lives in the water and on the land, too.

A **beaver's** fur is used on coats.

(beavers)

beaver
bea-ver
beaver

It is warm **because** the sun is shining.

Because tells why.

because
be-cause
because

A
B
C
D
E
F
G
H
I
J
K
L
M
N
O
P
Q
R
S
T
U
V
W
X
Y
Z

become
be-come
become

If you drink milk,

you will become strong and healthy.
grow to be

(becomes   became   becoming)

---

bed
bed

We sleep in a **bed.**
(beds)

---

bedroom
bed-room
bedroom

The room we sleep in
is a **bedroom.**

My bed is in my **bedroom.**
(bedrooms)

---

bedtime
bed-time
bedtime

Mother said it was bedtime.
time to go to bed.

---

bee
bee

This is a **bee.**

Bees make honey.
(bees)

---

been
been

"Some one has **been** sleeping in my bed,"
said the father bear.
(be   being)

---

beet
beet

This is a big red **beet.**

Mother cooked **beets** for dinner.
(beets)

---

before
be-fore
before

I wash my hands **before** I eat.

I wash my hands after I eat, too.

This dog wants something to eat. See him **beg** / ask for it. (begs begged begging)	**beg** *beg*
The sky grew black and it **began** / started to rain. (begin begins beginning begun)	**began** be-gan *began*
The teacher said, "Mary may **begin** / start the story." (begins began beginning begun)	**begin** be-gin *begin*
The boy sits **behind** / back of the girl.	**behind** be-hind *behind*
Mother gave Baby an apple for **being** good. (be been)	**being** be-ing *being*
I do not **believe** / think it is snowing. (believes believed believing)	**believe** be-lieve *believe*
Hear the **bell** ring. (bells)	**bell** *bell*
The book is not mine. It **belongs** to Bob. It is his. (belongs belonged belonging)	**belong** be-long *belong*

A Ⓑ C D E F G H I J K L M N O P Q R S T U V W X Y Z

below
be-low
below

The sun is high above.
The ground is down **below**.

belt
belt

This is Father's **belt**.
He wears it around his waist.
(belts)

bench
bench

Father's work bench

A bench to sit on
(benches)

bend
bend

The wire was not straight.
Bob tried to **bend** it
so that it would be straight.
(bends   bent   bending)

beneath
be-neath
beneath

The stool is **beneath** the window.
below

berry
ber-ry
berry

Strawberry   Raspberry   Blackberry

Berries are good to eat.
(berries)

Along came a spider And sat down beside her, by the side of And frightened Miss Muffet away.	**beside** be-side *beside*
Mary reads well. Bob reads better than Mary. Jack reads **best** of all.	**best** *best*
Bob reads **better** than Mary.	**better** bet-ter *better*
Mary walked **between** her mother and father.	**between** be-tween *between*
I stopped at the first store. Bob went **beyond.** further.	**beyond** be-yond *beyond*
Bob is riding his **bicycle.** (bicycles)	**bicycle** bi-cy-cle *bicycle*
Baby is **big.** not little. (bigger biggest)	**big** *big*
The bird eats with its **bill.** Mother paid our gas **bill.** A dollar **bill** is money. (bills)	**bill** *bill*

A
B
C
D
E
F
G
H
I
J
K
L
M
N
O
P
Q
R
S
T
U
V
W
X
Y
Z

A
B
C
D
E
F
G
H
I
J
K
L
M
N
O
P
Q
R
S
T
U
V
W
X
Y
Z

bird *bird*	This **bird** can fly high. (birds)
bird cage *bird cage*	The bird is in the **bird cage.** (bird cages)
birdhouse bird–house *birdhouse*	Bob made this **birdhouse.** Some birds build their nests in **birdhouses.** (birdhouses)
birthday birth-day *birthday*	This is my **birthday** cake. I am six years old today. (birthdays)
bit *bit*	Bobby gave Jane a **bit** of candy. small piece I **bit** into the cooky. (bite bites biting bitten)
bite *bite*	Baby has two teeth but she cannot **bite** you. (bites bit biting bitten)
bitter bit-ter *bitter*	The doctor left some medicine for Bob. Bob did not like it because it was **bitter.**
black *black*	This square is **black.** Coal is **black** and hard. Coal is dug out of the ground. (blacker blackest)

This is a **blackberry**.

Blackberries grow on bushes.

They are good to eat.

(blackberries)

blackberry
black-ber-ry
blackberry

See the **blackbird** in the tree.

Some **blackbirds** have red wings.

(blackbirds)

blackbird
black-bird
blackbird

The teacher writes on the **blackboard** with chalk.

The **blackboard** is black.

(blackboards)

cat dog

blackboard
black-board
blackboard

The **blade** of the knife is sharp.

We cut with the **blade** of a knife.

These are | **blades** | of grass.
　　　　　 | leaves |

(blades)

blade
blade

The man did not drive well.

He was | to **blame** | for the accident.
　　　　 | at fault |

(blames　blamed　blaming)

blame
blame

The | **blanket** | on your bed
　　 | cover |

keeps you warm.

Blankets are made of wool or cotton.

(blankets)

blanket
blan-ket
blanket

A
(B)
C
D
E
F
G
H
I
J
K
L
M
N
O
P
Q
R
S
T
U
V
W
X
Y
Z

blaze
blaze

The Indians watch the **blaze** of the fire.
bright light

The fire **blazes** high into the air.
burns

(blazes   blazed   blazing)

---

blew
blew

The wind **blew** the leaves off the trees.

Bob **blew** the whistle.
(blow   blows   blowing   blown)

---

blind
blind

The man is **blind.**
cannot see.

---

blocks
blocks

These are A B C **blocks.**

(block)

---

blood
blood

Mother cut her finger.
Red **blood** came from the cut.

---

bloom
bloom

Flowers **bloom** in the spring.
come out of buds

(blooms   bloomed   blooming)

---

blossom
blos-som
blossom

This is a **blossom.**
flower.

Fruit trees have **blossoms.**

Flowers **blossom** in the spring.
come out of buds

(blossoms   blossomed   blossoming)

Bob will **blow** the whistle. The wind **blows** the leaves from the trees. (blows blew blowing blown)	**blow** *blow*
The colors of the American flag are red, white, and **blue.**	**blue** *blue*
This bird is a **bluebird.** He has an orange-colored breast. (bluebirds)	**bluebird** blue-bird *bluebird*
This bird is a **blue jay.** The **blue jay's** back is blue. He has a knot of feathers on the top of his head. (blue jays)	**blue jay** *blue jay*
The man made a box of wide **boards.** **Boards** are made of wood. (board)	**boards** *boards*
Some people like to **boast.** talk about themselves too much. (boasts boasted boasting)	**boast** *boast*
This **boat** is large. People can cross the water on this **boat.** (boats)	**boat** *boat*

A
B
C
D
E
F
G
H
I
J
K
L
M
N
O
P
Q
R
S
T
U
V
W
X
Y
Z

body
bod-y
body

This is a doll's **body.**

Boys and girls have **bodies,** too.

You should keep your **body** clean.

(bodies)

---

boil
boil

Mary has a | **boil** | on her arm.
            | sore |

Mother put the water on the fire.

When it gets very hot,

it will | **boil.**
        | steam and bubble.

(boils   boiled   boiling)

---

bone
bone

The dog likes to eat a **bone.**

We have **bones** in our bodies.

(bones)

---

bonnet
bon-net
bonnet

Mother put the **bonnet** on the baby's head.

(bonnets)

---

book
book

This is a **book.**

I have a good **book** to read.

(books)

---

bookcase
book-case
bookcase

The books are in the **bookcase.**

(bookcases)

We played store.

I was the **bookkeeper**.

I wrote in the books how much **money we spent** and how much we took in.

(bookkeepers)

bookkeeper
book-keep-er
bookkeeper

We buy books

at the **bookstore.**
place where books are sold.

(bookstores)

bookstore
book-store
bookstore

The man has on rubber **boots**.
Boots are made of leather, too.
A **boot** is higher than a shoe.

(boots)

boot
boot

Mary's handkerchief

has a dark **border.**
edge.

(borders)

border
bor-der
border

We have a new baby at our house.

She was **born** yesterday.
brought into the world

born
born

The baby broke **both** her dolls.
her two

Baby closed **both** her eyes.

both
both

Bob lost his hat.

He did not **bother** to look for it.
take the trouble

(bothers   bothered   bothering)

bother
both-er
bother

A
B
C
D
E
F
G
H
I
J
K
L
M
N
O
P
Q
R
S
T
U
V
W
X
Y
Z

bottle
bot-tle
bottle

This is a **bottle**.

Milk is put into **bottles**.

Bottles are made of glass.

(bottles)

bottom
bot-tom
bottom

The picture is at the top of the page.

The story is at the **bottom** of
the page.

(bottoms)

bough
bough

The bird is sitting on a **bough** of the tree.
branch

(boughs)

bought
bought

Father gave Tom a penny.

Tom **bought** some candy with it.

(buy   buys   buying)

bounce
bounce

Mary likes to **bounce** the ball.

(bounces   bounced   bouncing)

bow
bow

Jack has a **bow** and arrow.

The **bow** is made with
a stick and a string.

Mary has a **bow** of ribbon
on her hair.

(bows)

Bob sang a song.

When the children clapped their hands, he made a **bow**.

(bows   bowed   bowing)

bow
bow

This is a **bowl**.

Baby eats from a **bowl**.

(bowls)

bowl
bowl

The dog said, "**Bow-wow**."

bow-wow
bow-wow
bow-wow

This is a **box**.

It has a lid on it.

(boxes)

box
box

Father is a big man.

Tom is a small **boy**.

(boys)

boy
boy

Children eat **bran**.

It is a breakfast food made from wheat and rye.

bran
bran

The bird is on a | **branch** | of the tree.
              | bough |

(branches)

branch
branch

Brass is hard like gold.

It is yellow, too.

Bowls are sometimes made of **brass**.

brass
brass

A
B
C
D
E
F
G
H
I
J
K
L
M
N
O
P
Q
R
S
T
U
V
W
X
Y
Z

A
B
C
D
E
F
G
H
I
J
K
L
M
N
O
P
Q
R
S
T
U
V
W
X
Y
Z

brave
brave

The soldier was **brave.**
not afraid.

(braver   bravest)

bread
bread

This is a loaf of **bread.**

One slice of **bread** has been cut.

break
break

Did you **break** the bowl?
(breaks   broke   breaking   broken)

breakfast
break-fast
breakfast

When I get up in the morning,
I eat my **breakfast.**

It is the first meal of the day.
(breakfasts)

breast
breast

The robin has a red **breast.**
(breasts)

breath
breath

To blow out a candle,
blow your **breath** against it.

breathe
breathe

You should **breathe** through your nose.
take in air

When you run, you **breathe** fast.
(breathes   breathed   breathing)

A **breeze** is blowing in the window.
wind

(breezes)

breeze
breeze

This house is made of **bricks**.

(brick)

bricks
bricks

The **bridge** is over the river.

We ride across the **bridge**.

(bridges)

bridge
bridge

The sun is **bright.**
shiny.

(brighter   brightest   brightly)

bright
bright

Mother went to the store.

She said, "I will **bring** you an apple."

(brings   brought   bringing)

bring
bring

This book is narrow.   This one is **broad.**
wide.

(broader   broadest)

broad
broad

The announcer will **broadcast**
send out
the news by radio.

(broadcasts   broadcasting)

broadcast
broad-cast
broadcast

A B C D E F G H I J K L M N O P Q R S T U V W X Y Z

A B C D E F G H I J K L M N O P Q R S T U V W X Y Z

broiling
broil-ing
broiling

Bob is **broiling** the meat
cooking

over the fire.

(broil   broils   broiled)

broke
broke

Mother dropped the dish and **broke** it.

(break   breaks   breaking   broken)

brook
brook

Father went fishing

in the **brook.**
small stream.

(brooks)

broom
broom

We sweep with a **broom.**

(brooms)

brother
broth-er
brother

The man is Jack's father.

The woman is Jack's mother.

The girl is Jack's sister.

The boy is Jack's **brother.**

(brothers)

brought
brought

Mother asked Bob to bring her a book.

Bob **brought** her a new book.

(bring   brings   bringing)

Leaves turn **brown** in autumn.

Bob has blue eyes.

Mary has **brown** eyes.

brown
brown

This is a **brownie**.

Brownies are funny little fellows.

(brownies)

brownie
brown-ie
brownie

A toothbrush   A scrub brush   A paint brush

I **brush** my teeth every day.

Do you?

(brushes   brushed   brushing)

brush
brush

This is a **bucket** of water.
pail

(buckets)

bucket
buck-et
bucket

A bud   A flower

When the **bud** opens, it will be a flower.

(buds)

bud
bud

This is a doll **buggy**.

(buggies)

buggy
bug-gy
buggy

A
B
C
D
E
F
G
H
I
J
K
L
M
N
O
P
Q
R
S
T
U
V
W
X
Y
Z

bugs
bugs

These are **bugs.**
(bug)

build
build

Men **build** houses.   Birds **build** nests.
(builds   built   building)

bulb
bulb

Bob is planting a lily **bulb.**
Some plants grow from seeds.
Some grow from **bulbs.**
This is an electric light **bulb.**
(bulbs)

bulletin
bul-le-tin
bulletin

"It is raining today.
It will snow tomorrow.
It will be colder tomorrow."

This is a **bulletin** telling about the weather.
message
(bulletins)

bumped
bumped

Baby fell down.

She **bumped** her head.
hit

It made a big **bump** on her head.
(bump   bumps   bumping)

Mother made some **buns** | rolls
for dinner.
Some **buns** are like cake and some are like bread.
(bun)

buns
buns

One flower   **A bunch of flowers**

One grape   **A bunch** of grapes
(bunches)

bunch
bunch

This is Bob's **bunny.** | pet rabbit.
(bunnies)

bunny
bun-ny
bunny

The house is on fire.
It may **burn** down.
(burns   burned   burning)

burn
burn

Dogs **bury** | place bones in the ground.

When they get hungry, they dig them up
and eat them.
(buries   buried   burying)

bury
bur-y
bury

This is a big **bus.**
Many people ride in a **bus.**
(buses)

bus
bus

A B C D E F G H I J K L M N O P Q R S T U V W X Y Z

bush
bush

Apples grow on a tree.

Roses grow on a **bush.**

A tree is bigger than a **bush.**

(bushes)

busy
bus-y
busy

Tom worked all day.

Father said, "What a **busy** boy you are!"

(busier   busiest   business)

but
but

The fox wanted the grapes,

but he could not get them.

butcher
but-cher
butcher

This man is a **butcher.**

He has a meat market.

He cuts and sells meat.

(butchers)

butter
but-ter
butter

Bread and **butter** are good
to eat.

Butter is made from cream.

buttercup
but-ter-cup
buttercup

This flower is a **buttercup.**

Buttercups are yellow.

(buttercups)

butterfly
but-ter-fly
butterfly

A butterfly

Butterflies have bright colors.

They grow from caterpillars.

(butterflies)

Butter is made from cream.

The milk that is left from the cream
   is called **buttermilk.**

Buttermilk is good to drink.

buttermilk
but-ter-milk
buttermilk

I can **button** my dress.

These are **buttons.**

Some **buttons** are flat and round.
Buttons are pretty on dresses.

   (buttons   buttoned   buttoning)

button
but-ton
button

Father gave Bob a nickel to **buy** candy.

     See him **buying** candy
       with the money.

    (buys   bought   buying)

buy
buy

Dogs say, "Bow-wow!"

Robins say, "Cheer-up, Cheer-up."

Bees say, **"Buzz buzz."**

(buzzes buzzed buzzing)

buzz
buzz

The man is standing

   | **by** | the tree.
   | at the side of |

The kite was made **by** Father.

Father made it.

by
by

A
B
C
D
E
F
G
H
I
J
K
L
M
N
O
P
Q
R
S
T
U
V
W
X
Y
Z

cabbage
cab-bage
cabbage

This is a head of **cabbage.**

Some **cabbages** are white and some are red.

Cabbage is good to eat.

(cabbages)

cage
cage

A bird is in this **cage.**

We saw a lion in a **cage** at the circus.

(cages)

cake
cake

A round cake

A square cake

(cakes)

calendar
cal-en-dar
calendar

This is a **calendar.**

It helps to tell which month and day it is.

(calendars)

calf
calf

This is a cow and her baby **calf.**

(calves)

call
call

Jack did not hear his mother's **call.**

She **called** him again and again.

(calls   called   calling)

54

John called his dog.
The dog **came** to him.
(come   comes   coming)

came
came

This is a **camel**.
Camels can travel a long time without drinking water.
(camels)

camel
cam-el
camel

This is a **camera**.
We take pictures with a **camera**.
(cameras)

camera
cam-er-a
camera

Father and I like to | **camp**
| live |
by the roadside in a tent.

Boy Scouts like to | **camp** out.
| live outdoors. |

These people are **camping**.
(camps   camped   camping)

camp
camp

An oil can   A garbage **can**   A coffee can

I | **can** | make a kite.
| am able to |

Mother | **cans** | fruit in jars.
| puts |

(cans   canned   canning)

can
can

A B C D E F G H I J K L M N O P Q R S T U V W X Y Z

55

A
B
C
D
E
F
G
H
I
J
K
L
M
N
O
P
Q
R
S
T
U
V
W
X
Y
Z

Canada
Ca-na-da
Canada

Canada is
a big country.

Here is a map
of **Canada.**

(Canadian)

CANADA
U. S. A.

candle
can-dle
candle

This is a **candle.**

Mother put six **candles** on my birthday cake.

(candles)

candlestick
can-dle-stick
candlestick

This candle is in a **candlestick.**
holder for a candle.

(candlesticks)

candy
can-dy
candy

Sticks of candy   A box of candy

Candy is sweet.

(candies)

cane
cane

The man walks with a **cane.**

(canes)

cannot
can-not
cannot

Birds can fly.

Dogs **cannot** fly.

canoe
ca-noe
canoe

This boat is called a **canoe.**

Indians used **canoes.**

(canoes)

Dogs **can't** fly. / cannot	**can't** *can't*	A B **C** D E F G H I J K L M N O P Q R S T U V W X Y Z

Dogs **can't** fly.
cannot

can't
can't

Bob wears a **cap** on his head.
(caps)

cap
cap

Mary made a **cape** for her doll.
(capes)

cape
cape

We call the leader of our team our **captain.**
(captains)

captain
cap-tain
captain

Automobile   Freight car

These are **cars.**
(cars)

car
car

A postcard   A playing card

These are **cards.**
(cards)

card
card

Mother takes **care** of the baby.
looks after

I do not **care** to play.
want

(cares   cared   caring)

care
care

careful
care-ful
careful

Bob cut his hand with a knife.

He was not **careful.**

(carefully)

carriage
car-riage
carriage

The princess rode in a **carriage** drawn by horses.

(carriages)

carrot
car-rot
carrot

A carrot

Carrots are good to eat.

Carrots are orange in color.

(carrots)

carry
car-ry
carry

Father will **carry** ~~take~~ the baby in his arms.

(carries   carried   carrying)

cart
cart

Bobby is pulling the **cart.**

It has two wheels.

(carts)

case
case

A suitcase   A showcase   A bookcase

We put things in **cases.**

(cases)

A castle

(castles)

castle
cas-tle
castle

I call my **cat** "Fluffy."

(cats)

cat
cat

Bob is throwing the ball.

Tom will **catch** it.

(catches   caught   catching)

catch
catch

Here is a **caterpillar**.

Caterpillars turn into butterflies.

(caterpillars)

caterpillar
cat-er-pil-lar
caterpillar

This plant is a **cattail**.

The leaves are green.

The tail is brown.

Cattails grow in a wet place.

(cattails)

cattail
cat-tail
cattail

These are some of the animals
    that live on a farm.

They are called **cattle**.

cattle
cat-tle
cattle

A broken wheel | **caused** the car to | run
             | made the car |

into the post.

(cause   causes   causing)

caused
caused

A
B
©
D
E
F
G
H
I
J
K
L
M
N
O
P
Q
R
S
T
U
V
W
X
Y
Z

cave *cave*	The boys dug a big hole in the side of the hill. They left a little door to get in. They called it their **cave.** (caves)
caw *caw*	The robin says, "Cheer-up, Cheer-up." The crow says, **"Caw-caw-caw."** (caws cawed cawing)
celery cel-er-y *celery*	**Celery** is good to eat. **Celery** is covered up while it is growing. This makes it white.
cent *cent*	Grandmother gave me one | **cent** / penny | to buy candy.
center cen-ter *center*	The cross is in the | **center** / middle | of the ring. (centers)
cereal ce-re-al *cereal*	We should eat **cereal** for breakfast. **Cereal** is made from grain. (cereals)
certain cer-tain *certain*	Bob was not | **certain** / sure | that he could go. (certainly)

There is **a chain**
across the road.

(chains)

chain
chain

A kitchen chair   **An** armchair

(chairs)

chair
chair

I wrote on the blackboard
with **chalk.**

mother

chalk
chalk

Tom won all the games.

He was the **champion.**

(champions)

champion
cham-pi-on
champion

Mary likes to swim whenever she has a **chance** to.

(chances)

chance
chance

Bob got his shoes wet.

He had to **change** his wet shoes
for dry ones.

(changes   changed   changing)

change
change

Bob is a **character** in the play.
an actor

(characters)

character
char-ac-ter
character

A B C D E F G H I J K L M N O P Q R S T U V W X Y Z

A
B
C
D
E
F
G
H
I
J
K
L
M
N
O
P
Q
R
S
T
U
V
W
X
Y
Z

chart
chart

Father is looking
at the **chart.**

(charts)

chase
chase

The dog likes to **chase** the cat.
run after

(chases   chased   chasing)

cheap
cheap

Mother bought a new dress for me.

It was **cheap.**
did not cost much money.

(cheaper   cheapest)

checks
checks

This cloth has **checks** in it.
squares

(check)

cheek
cheek

Baby put her hand
on her **cheek.**

(cheeks)

cheer
cheer

Our team won the game.

We all gave a loud **cheer.**
shout.

(cheers   cheered   cheering)

cheerful
cheer-ful
cheerful

The children were **cheerful.**
happy.

(cheerfully)

Mice like to eat **cheese.**

I like **cheese,** too.

It is made from milk.

cheese
cheese

Cherries are red.

They grow on trees.

(cherry)

cherries
cher-ries
cherries

The boy put his hand on his **chest.**

This is a **chest** for clothes.

(chests)

chest
chest

Did you ever see a toasted **chestnut?**
Chestnuts grow on **chestnut** trees.

They are big brown nuts.

(chestnuts)

chestnut
chest-nut
chestnut

Baby put the cracker into her mouth.

Father told her to **chew** it well.

(chews   chewed   chewing)

chew
chew

A baby chick

(chicks)

chick
chick

A **chickadee** is a small bird.

(chickadees)

chickadee
chick-a-dee
chickadee

A
B
C
D
E
F
G
H
I
J
K
L
M
N
O
P
Q
R
S
T
U
V
W
X
Y
Z

chicken
chick-en
chicken

A chicken

(chickens)

chief
chief

This is an Indian | **chief.**
| leader.

(chiefs)

child
child

This girl is a little **child.**

(children)

children
chil-dren
children

These are **children.**

(child)

chimney
chim-ney
chimney

A chimney

Smoke goes out the **chimney.**

(chimneys)

chin
chin

The boy is reading with his **chin**
on his hand.

(chins)

china
chi-na
china

This is a **china** cup.

China
Chi-na
China

This man came from **China.**

China is a country on the other side
of the world.

(Chinese)

64

The **chipmunk** is running up the tree.
He is a kind of squirrel.
(chipmunks)

chipmunk
chip-munk
chipmunk

Bob picked up | chips | of wood
| small pieces |

to make a fire.
(chip)

chips
chips

A bar of
chocolate

A chocolate
cake

A cup of
hot chocolate

chocolate
choc-o-late
chocolate

The children went to play a game.

The leader will | **choose** | the children to play.
| pick out |

(chooses   chose   choosing)

choose
choose

The woodcutter will | **chop** | down the tree
| cut |

with an ax.
(chops   chopped   chopping)

A pork chop

chop
chop

The leader | **chose** | Bob to play in the game.
| picked out |

(choose   chooses   choosing)

chose
chose

A Christmas tree

December 25 is **Christmas** day.

Christmas is Christ's birthday.

Christmas
Christ-mas
Christmas

A B C D E F G H I J K L M N O P Q R S T U V W X Y Z

A
B
©
D
E
F
G
H
I
J
K
L
M
N
O
P
Q
R
S
T
U
V
W
X
Y
Z

church *church*		I go to **church.** (churches)
churn *churn*	Bob helps Grandmother **churn** / beat the butter from the cream. The machine for making butter is called a **churn.** (churns churned churning)	
cigar ci-gar *cigar*		The man is smoking a **cigar.** (cigars)
circle cir-cle *circle*		This is a **circle.** / ring. (circles)
circus cir-cus *circus*	The children went to the **circus.** They saw the elephants and the clowns at the **circus.** (circuses)	
citizen cit-i-zen *citizen*	Many people live in the United States. These people are called **citizens.** The laws make the country a safe place for **citizens** to live in. I am a **citizen** of the United States. (citizens citizenship)	

The farmer lives in the country.

I live in a | **city.**
| large town. |

(cities)

city

cit-y

city

Mary liked the music.

See her **clap** her hands.

(claps clapped clapping)

clap

clap

Bob and Mary go to school.

Bob is in a higher | **class** | than Mary.
| grade |

(classes)

class

class

A **claw** is like a fingernail.

The cat has sharp **claws.**

She scratches the rug with her **claws.**

(claws)

claw

claw

Mary made a bowl from | **clay.**
| mud. |

clay

clay

Mother will | **clean** | the house.
| get the dirt out of |

Mother said, "Wash your hands **clean**
with soap and warm water."

(cleans cleaned cleaning)
(cleaner cleanest)

clean

clean

This man is a street **cleaner.**

He makes the streets clean.

(cleaners)

cleaner

clean-er

cleaner

A
B
C
D
E
F
G
H
I
J
K
L
M
N
O
P
Q
R
S
T
U
V
W
X
Y
Z

clear *clear*	The water has dirt in it. It is not **clear**. (clearer clearest clearly)
clerk *clerk*	Mary is a **clerk** in a store. She sells books and paper. (clerks)
climb *climb*	Bob can **climb** go up the tree. (climbs climbed climbing)
clip *clip*	This is a paper **clip**. It is used to hold papers together. (clips)
clock *clock*	The **clock** tells us what time it is. (clocks)
close *close*	Mary is too **close** near to the railroad track. (closer closest)
close *close*	It is cold. Bob will **close** shut the door. (closes closed closing)
cloth *cloth*	Mother bought some pretty **cloth**.

Mother hung the **clothes** on the clothesline.	**clothes** *clothes*
See the towels on the **clothesline.** The **clothesline** is a strong rope. (clotheslines)	**clothesline** clothes-line *clothesline*
I see a big **cloud** in the sky. (clouds cloudy)	**cloud** *cloud*
A clover leaf A clover blossom (clovers)	**clover** clo-ver *clover*
I saw a **clown** at the circus. (clowns)	**clown** *clown*
This is a **club.** heavy stick. Some men belong to golf **clubs.** (clubs)	**club** *club*
The hen said, "Cluck! Cluck! Cluck!"	**cluck** *cluck*
The king rode in a **coach** carriage drawn by horses. (coaches)	**coach** *coach*

A
B
Ⓒ
D
E
F
G
H
I
J
K
L
M
N
O
P
Q
R
S
T
U
V
W
X
Y
Z

coal
coal

The bucket is filled with coal.

coast
coast

The children like to [coast slide downhill] on their sleds.

(coasts   coasted   coasting)

Some people live on the [coast. seashore.]

coat
coat

Bobby is putting on his **coat.**

(coats)

cock
cock

This [cock rooster] crows in the morning.

(cocks)

cock-a-doodle-doo
cock-a-doo-dle-doo
cock-a-doodle-doo

The rooster says, "**Cock-a-doodle-doo.**"

cocoa
cocoa

Children drink **cocoa.**

It makes them big and strong.

cocoon
co-coon
cocoon

A butterfly will come out of this **cocoon.**

(cocoons)

Some children drink milk. It helps them grow. Some children drink **coffee.** It does not help them grow.	**coffee** cof-fee *coffee*
The sun makes us warm. The snow makes us **cold.** (colder coldest)	**cold** *cold*
Father put a **collar** around the dog's neck. This is the **collar** of a man's **shirt.** (collars)	**collar** col-lar *collar*
My brother goes to college. school. (colleges)	**college** col-lege *college*
We color Easter eggs. paint Red, yellow, and blue are **colors.** (colors colored coloring)	**color** col-or *color*
A mother horse and her baby **colt.** (colts)	**colt** *colt*
Mary uses a **comb** to **comb** her hair. (combs combed combing)	**comb** *comb*

A
B
Ⓒ
D
E
F
G
H
I
J
K
L
M
N
O
P
Q
R
S
T
U
V
W
X
Y
Z

A
B
C
D
E
F
G
H
I
J
K
L
M
N
O
P
Q
R
S
T
U
V
W
X
Y
Z

come
come

Tom's dog will **come**
whenever he is called.
(comes   came   coming)

company
com-pa-ny
company

Some children came to our house.
They were our **company**.

complete
com-plete
complete

Bob wants to **complete** his picture
finish

before lunch.
(completes   completed   completing)

conductor
con-duc-tor
conductor

This man is a **conductor**.
He takes the tickets or money
for our ride.
(conductors)

cone
cone

An ice cream **cone**
is good to eat.

A pine **cone**
grows on a pine tree.
(cones)

cook
cook

This man is a **cook**.
He will **cook** dinner for you.
(cooks   cooked   cooking)

cooky
cook-y
cooky

Jack ate a **cooky**.
It had a raisin in it.
(cookies)

It is **cool** today.
not warm

(cooler   coolest)
(cools   cooled   cooling)

cool
cool

Bob tried to **copy** Mary's picture.
make a picture just like Mary's.

(copies   copied   copying)

copy
cop-y
copy

An ear of corn

corn
corn

The corn has been eaten.

This is the **corncob**.
(corncobs)

corncob
corn-cob
corncob

Little Jack Horner

Sat in a **corner**.
(corners)

corner
cor-ner
corner

Mother bought a **new dress**.

It **cost** twenty dollars.
(costs   costing)

cost
cost

This small house is a **cottage**.

We live in a **cottage** by the sea.
(cottages)

cottage
cot-tage
cottage

This is a **cotton** plant.

Some clothes are made from **cotton**.

cotton
cot-ton
cotton

A B C D E F G H I J K L M N O P Q R S T U V W X Y Z

A B C D E F G H I J K L M N O P Q R S T U V W X Y Z

cough *cough*	Mary is sick with a cold. She has a bad **cough.** (coughs coughed coughing)
could *could*	Bob could reach the cooky jar. was able to
couldn't *couldn't*	I couldn't read the story. could not was not able to
count *count*	1, 2, 3, 4, 5, 6, 7, 8, 9, 10. Can you **count** to 10? (counts counted counting)

country coun-try *country*	Bob lives in the city,
	   but Tom lives on a farm
	   in the **country.**
	
	Mary lives in Canada, but Helen lives in another
	   country.
	
	(countries)

course *course*	Of course I will go. Surely
court *court*	The man stole the money. The policeman took him to **court.** (courts)

Bob and Mary are my aunt's children.

Bob is my **cousin.**

Mary is my **cousin,** too.

(cousins)

cousin
cous-in
cousin

Mother will **cover** the baby
with a blanket.

She will put a blanket over her.

A can with a cover   The cover of a can

(covers   covered   covering)

cover
cov-er
cover

This is a **cow.**

Cows give us milk.

(cows)

cow
cow

The cow sleeps in the **cow barn.**

(cow barns)

cow barn
cow barn

A cowboy

(cowboys)

cowboy
cow-boy
cowboy

This bowl has a **crack** in it.

Bob will **crack** some nuts.

(cracks   cracked   cracking)

crack
crack

A B C D E F G H I J K L M N O P Q R S T U V W X Y Z

cracker
crack-er
cracker

Polly wants a **cracker.**

(crackers)

cradle
cra-dle
cradle

This is a doll's **cradle.** bed with rockers.

(cradles)

cranberry
cran-ber-ry
cranberry

We ate **cranberry** sauce with our turkey. **Cranberries** are red.

(cranberries)

crawl
crawl

The baby cannot walk

but she can **crawl.** creep.

(crawls   crawled   crawling)

crayon
cray-on
crayon

I like to color pictures with colored **crayons.**

A box of crayons

One crayon

(crayons)

cream
cream

Mother has whipped some **cream.**
It will make dessert taste even better.

Baby cannot walk but she can | creep.
crawl.

(creeps   crept   creeping)

creep
creep

Put a **cross** after your name.

Bob | will **cross** | the street.
go across

(crosses   crossed   crossing)

cross
cross

This bird is a big black **crow.**
(crows)

crow
crow

One boy and one girl   A crowd of children

All the boys tried to | **crowd**
push

through the door at once.

The room is | **crowded.**
filled very full.

(crowds   crowded   crowding)

crowd
crowd

The king's crown
(crowns)

crown
crown

The man is very **cruel.**
He likes to see others in pain.

cruel
cru-el
cruel

Birds eat | **crumbs** | of bread.
small pieces

(crumb)

crumbs
crumbs

A
B
C
D
E
F
G
H
I
J
K
L
M
N
O
P
Q
R
S
T
U
V
W
X
Y
Z

cry *cry*	The rabbit could not get the goats out of the turnip patch. The bee said, "Do not **cry.** I will get them out for you." (cries cried crying)
cup *cup*	Jane drinks out of a **cup.** (cups)
cupboard cup-board *cupboard*	Old Mother Hubbard Went to the **cupboard.** (cupboards)
cure *cure*	If you are sick, the doctor will **cure** you. make you well. (cures cured curing)
curling iron curl-ing i-ron *curlingiron*	Mother curls Mary's hair with a **curling iron.** (curling irons)
curls *curls*	Mary has her hair in **curls.** Her mother **curls** it for her on a **curling** iron. (curl curled curling)

Mother is putting up the **curtain** at the window.

(curtains)

curtain
cur-tain
curtain

A straight line   A curved line

(curve   curves   curving)

curved
curved

This is a | **cushion.** |
| pillow. |

(cushions)

cushion
cush-ion
cushion

Tom **cut** his hand with a knife.

(cuts   cutting)

cut
cut

The baby is | **cute.** |
| little and pretty. |

(cuter   cutest)

cute
cute

A B C D E F G H I J K L M N O P Q R S T U V W X Y Z

A
B
C
D
E
F
G
H
I
J
K
L
M
N
O
P
Q
R
S
T
U
V
W
X
Y
Z

dad *dad*	Some children call their father **Dad.** (dads daddy)
dairy dair-y *dairy*	They sell milk and butter at the **dairy.** (dairies)
daisy dai-sy *daisy*	This flower is a **daisy.** It is white with a yellow center. (daisies)
dance *dance*	The children like to **dance.** (dances danced dancing)
dandelion dan-de-li-on *dandelion*	This flower is a **dandelion.** **Dandelions** are yellow. (dandelions)
danger dan-ger *danger*	Do not cross the street when the light is red. It means **danger.** you may get hurt. (dangerous)
dare *dare*	Bob said, "I **dare** you to jump into the lake." (dares dared daring)
dark *dark*	At night the sky is **dark.** not light. (darker darkest)
dashed *dashed*	The man **dashed** to the fire. hurried (dash dashes dashing)

Have you eaten a **date?**

The **date** of my birthday is May 5.

(dates)

date
date

A boy is a son of his mother and father.

A girl is a **daughter** of her mother and father.

(daughters)

daughter
daugh-ter
daughter

What is the first **day** of the week?

Monday and Tuesday are two of the **days.**

(days)

day
day

My mother is **dear** to me.

I love her very much.

(dears   dearly)

dear
dear

December is the twelfth month
of the year.

December
De-cem-ber
December

Father will **decide** whether to have a picnic.
make up his mind

(decides   decided   deciding)

decide
de-cide
decide

Bob can dig a **deep** hole
in the ground.

(deeper   deepest)

deep
deep

A **deer**

deer
deer

A B C **D** E F G H I J K L M N O P Q R S T U V W X Y Z

delight
de-light
delight

Father takes | **delight** / great joy | in surprising the children.
(delights   delighted   delighting)

delivers
de-liv-ers
delivers

The postman | **delivers** / brings | letters to our house.
(deliver   delivered   delivering)

demand
de-mand
demand

Father will | **demand** / ask | that you bring back our books.
(demands   demanded   demanding)

den
den

The fox went into his | **den.** / home.
(dens)

dentist
den-tist
dentist

The man is a **dentist.**
He fixes teeth.
(dentists)

describe
de-scribe
describe

Bob wanted to | **describe** / tell about | his visit to the farm.
(describes   described   describing)

desert
des-ert
desert

The camel travels
through the **desert.**
The **desert** is sandy land
without water and trees.
(deserts)

Helen does good work in school.

She **deserves** a good mark.
~~should have~~

(deserve   deserved   deserving)

deserves
de-serves
deserves

These are **desks**.
Which kind of **desk** do you have?

(desks)

desk
desk

The boy **destroyed** the paper.
tore up

Fire will **destroy** the house.
put an end to

(destroys   destroyed   destroying)

destroy
de-stroy
destroy

We found **dew** on the grass
drops of water

this morning.

dew
dew

Mother has a **diamond** ring.
The **diamond** sparkles.
(diamonds)

diamond
di-a-mond
diamond

A **dictionary** tells what words mean.
This book is a picture **dictionary**.

(dictionaries)

dictionary
dic-tion-ar-y
dictionary

The girl **did** her work well.
(do   does   done   doing)

did
did

A B C **D** E F G H I J K L M N O P Q R S T U V W X Y Z

didn't
didn't

The girl **didn't** do her work well.
did not

---

die
die

The mouse will **die** if the cat catches him.
stop living

(dies   died   dying   dead   death)

---

different
dif-fer-ent
different

This book is **different from** that one.
not like

(difference)

---

dig
dig

Bob can **dig** in the sand with his shovel.
(digs   dug   digging)

---

dime
dime

Ten pennies make a **dime.**

Two nickels make a **dime.**

(dimes)

---

ding
ding

Ding, dong bell,
Pussy's in the well.

---

dining
din-ing
dining

The children eat in the **dining** room.

---

dinner
din-ner
dinner

The children are eating **dinner.**
We have **dinner** at six o'clock.

(dinners)

The children were going north. That was the wrong **direction.** Bob made his picture right. He followed the teacher's **directions.** (directions)	**direction** di-rec-tion *direction*
Mary fell down. She got dirt mud on her dress.	**dirt** *dirt*
The children played in the sand. Their hands were dirty. not clean. (dirtier dirtiest)	**dirty** dirt-y *dirty*
The cat disappeared ran from sight up a tree. (disappear disappears disappearing)	**disappeared** dis-ap-peared *disappeared*
A **disease** is a kind of sickness. (diseases)	**disease** dis-ease *disease*
The **dishes** are on the table. (dish)	**dishes** dish-es *dishes*
A **dishwasher** cleans dishes. (dishwashers)	**dishwasher** dish-wash-er *dishwasher*
It is a long distance way from here to our school. (distances)	**distance** dis-tance *distance*

A B C **D** E F G H I J K L M N O P Q R S T U V W X Y Z

divide
di-vide
divide

Bob cut the apple in two.

He said, "I will **divide** my apple share
with you.

I will give you part of it."
(divides   divided   dividing)

do
do

I **do** my work well.
(does   did   doing   done)

doctor
doc-tor
doctor

Father is sick.

The **doctor** came to make him well.
(doctors)

does
does

Bob **does** his work well.
(do   did   doing   done)

dog
dog

The **dog** barks loudly.
(dogs)

doll
doll

This is a baby **doll**.
(dolls   dolly)

dollar
dol-lar
dollar

This is a **dollar** sign.

A **dollar** is 100 cents.
(dollars)

$

dollhouse
doll-house
dollhouse

The doll lives
in a **dollhouse**.
house made for dolls.
(dollhouses)

You may go home when your work is **done.**
finished.

(do   does   did   doing)

done
done

A donkey
(donkeys)

donkey
don-key
donkey

I **don't** sing well.
do not

don't
don't

The **door** is shut.
(doors)

door
door

Mary is ringing the **doorbell.**

Mother will go to the door.

(doorbells)

doorbell
door-bell
doorbell

Bob is sitting on the **doorstep.**
(doorsteps)

doorstep
door-step
doorstep

Mary is standing in the **doorway.**
(doorways)

doorway
door-way
doorway

This cloth has **dots** in it.
(dot)

dots
dots

We spell book with **double** o's.
two

(doubles   doubled   doubling)

double
dou-ble
double

A B C D E F G H I J K L M N O P Q R S T U V W X Y Z

dove
dove

This bird is a **dove.**

A **dove** is sometimes called a pigeon.

(doves)

down
down

The squirrel ran **down** the tree.

downstairs
down-stairs
downstairs

The boy is coming **downstairs.**
down the stairs.

downtown
down-town
downtown

Mother went **downtown** to buy a dress.

She went to the part of town where the stores are.

dozen
doz-en
dozen

Helen went to the store

to buy **a dozen** eggs.
twelve

drank
drank

The baby **drank** the milk.

(drink   drinks   drinking   drunk)

draw
draw

Tom can **draw** pictures.

(draws   drew   drawing   drawn)

dreadful
dread-ful
dreadful

"Something **dreadful** has happened,"
terrible

said the boy.

"The goats are in my turnip patch
and I can't get them out."

Bob had a **dream** when he was asleep. He **dreamed** he was riding on an elephant. (dreams dreamed dreaming)	**dream** *dream*
Mary is wearing a **dress**. (dresses)	**dress** *dress*
This is a **dresser**. We keep clothes in a **dresser**. (dressers)	**dresser** dres-ser *dresser*
We are giving a play. We will **drill on practice** our parts today. (drills drilled drilling)	**drill** *drill*
See Baby **drink** her milk. (drinks drank drinking drunk)	**drink** *drink*
Mary is getting a drink from the **drinking fountain**. (drinking fountains)	**drinking fountain** drink-ing foun-tain *drinking fountain*
This man **drives** the auto. He is the driver. He makes the car go. (drive drove driving driver)	**drives** *drives*

A
B
C
D
E
F
G
H
I
J
K
L
M
N
O
P
Q
R
S
T
U
V
W
X
Y
Z

driveway
drive-way
driveway

The car is standing

in the **driveway.**

(driveways)

---

drop
drop

A **drop** of rain fell on Mary's dress.

Did you see Mary **drop** a package?

(drops   dropped   dropping)

---

drown
drown

The cat fell into the water.

She could not swim.

I pulled her out

so she would not **drown.**
die under the water.

(drowns   drowned   drowning)

---

drug
drug

Father was sick.

Bob ran to the **drug**store

to get some **drugs** for him.
medicine

(drugs)

---

drum
drum

Bob likes to beat his **drum.**

(drums)

---

dry
dry

The rain makes the ground wet.

The sun makes the ground **dry.**

The sun **dries** the ground.

(dries   dried   drying)

A duck
(ducks)

duck
duck

A **duckling** is a baby duck.
(ducklings)

duckling
duck-ling
duckling

We ate apples | **during** | our play class.
| while we were having |

during
dur-ing
during

The wind blew | **dust** | into my eyes.
| fine dirt |

Mother **dusts** the furniture.

She rubs off the dust.
(dusts   dusted   dusting)

dust
dust

This is a little **Dutch** girl.

She lives in Holland.

Dutch
Dutch

This man did not grow big.

A **dwarf** is a little person.
(dwarfs)

dwarf
dwarf

We | **dwell** | in a brick house.
| live |

(dwells   dwelt   dwelling   dwelled)

dwell
dwell

The | **dwellers** | in this town are Americans.
| people who live |

(dweller)

dwellers
dwell-ers
dwellers

A
B
C
D
E
F
G
H
I
J
K
L
M
N
O
P
Q
R
S
T
U
V
W
X
Y
Z

each
each

I gave **each** boy one apple.

eager
ea-ger
eager

Bob | is **eager** | to see my kite.
| wants |

(eagerly)

eagle
ea-gle
eagle

This bird is an **eagle.**

He is very large.

(eagles)

ear
ear

We hear with our **ears.**

An ear   An ear of corn

(ears)

early
ear-ly
early

I started to school **early**
  so that I would not be late.

(earlier   earliest)

earned
earned

I have a dime.

I **earned** it by working for Father.

(earn   earns   earning)

earth
earth

The man puts the seeds

into the | **earth.** |
| ground. |

Our world is called the **earth.**

The sun comes up in the **east.**

(eastern)

east
east

We color eggs for **Easter.**

The flower is an **Easter** lily.

Easter
East-er
Easter

My book is **easy** to read.
not hard

(easier   easiest   easily)

easy
eas-y
easy

The boy will **eat** the apple.

(eats   ate   eating   eaten)

eat
eat

Bob put a line near the **edge**
of the paper.

(edges)

edge
edge

Birds lay **eggs.**

The **eggs** are in the nest.

Eggs are good to eat.

(egg)

eggs
eggs

Here are **eight** apples.
8

Count them.

(eighth   eighty)

8

eight
eight

A
B
C
D
(E)
F
G
H
I
J
K
L
M
N
O
P
Q
R
S
T
U
V
W
X
Y
Z

either
ei-ther
either

You may have **either** dog.
You may have this one or that one.

electric
e-lec-tric
electric

This is an **electric** light.
This is an **electric** iron.

electricity
e-lec-tric-i-ty
electricity

The electric iron is kept warm by **electricity.**

elephant
el-e-phant
elephant

I saw an **elephant** at the zoo.
Elephants are very big.
(elephants)

elevator
el-e-va-tor
elevator

The children went up
in the **elevator.**
(elevators)

eleven
e-lev-en
eleven

The boy saw **eleven** stars.
Count them.
(eleventh)

11

elf
elf

This is an **elf.**
An **elf** is like a fairy.
(elves)

else
else

Who **else** will come to my party?
What other persons

The box is **empty.**
has nothing in it.

Bob **emptied** the apples
took out all

from the basket.
(empties   emptied   emptying)

empty
emp-ty
empty

Mary is holding
one **end** of the rope.
Bob is holding
the other **end.**

The children were fighting.

Mother came and the fighting **ended.**
stopped.

(ends   ended   ending)

end
end

A soldier does not fight friends.

He fights the **enemy.**
people who are against him.

(enemies)

enemy
en-e-my
enemy

This is an **engine.**
It pulls railroad cars.
(engines   engineer)

engine
en-gine
engine

Did you **enjoy** the story?
Did the story make you happy?
(enjoys   enjoyed   enjoying)

enjoy
en-joy
enjoy

Mother had

enough apples for everyone.
as many apples as she needed.

enough
e-nough
enough

A
B
C
D
(E)
F
G
H
I
J
K
L
M
N
O
P
Q
R
S
T
U
V
W
X
Y
Z

A
B
C
D
(E)
F
G
H
I
J
K
L
M
N
O
P
Q
R
S
T
U
V
W
X
Y
Z

envelope en-ve-lope *envelope*	This is an **envelope**. We put letters in **envelopes**. (envelopes)
errand er-rand *errand*	Bob went to the store for Mother. Mary went on an **errand** for Mother, too. (errands)
escape es-cape *escape*	The lion is trying to **escape** from / get out of the cage. (escapes escaped escaping)
Eskimo Es-ki-mo *Eskimo*	This is an **Eskimo** mother. **Eskimos** live in the North. (Eskimos)
even e-ven *even*	Can you fold the paper so that the edges will be **even**? Bob's and Mary's pencils are **even**. / the same size. The boys divided the sand into **even** / equal piles. Mother **evened** / smoothed the frosting on the cake. (evens evened evening)
evening e-ven-ing *evening*	When the sun goes down, it is **evening**. After the **evening**, it is night. (evenings)

Did you **ever** see a cow? at any time	**ever** ev-er *ever*
I drink milk **every** day. each	**every** ev-er-y *every*
She gave **everybody** an apple. each person	**everybody** ev-er-y-bod-y *everybody*
She gave **everyone** an apple. everybody	**everyone** ev-er-y-one *everyone*
The boys put **everything** all the things into the box.	**everything** ev-er-y-thing *everything*
Mary looked **everywhere** for her doll. every place	**everywhere** ev-er-y-where *everywhere*
I go to school every day **except** Saturday and Sunday. but	**except** ex-cept *except*
My new shoes are too small. Mother will **exchange** them for a larger pair. Tom and Betty will **exchange** books. (exchanges exchanged exchanging)	**exchange** ex-change *exchange*

A B C D Ⓔ F G H I J K L M N O P Q R S T U V W X Y Z

97

A
B
C
D
(E)
F
G
H
I
J
K
L
M
N
O
P
Q
R
S
T
U
V
W
X
Y
Z

excited ex-cit-ed *excited*	The fire bell rang. The children were **excited**. (excite excites exciting)
excuse ex-cuse *excuse*	Mary is polite. She says "Excuse me," when she walks in front of you. The teacher will **excuse you** if you are sick. let you go Bob's father wrote an **excuse** to the teacher. (excuses excused excusing)
exercise ex-er-cise *exercise*	Playing ball is good **exercise**. Running is good **exercise**. (exercises exercised exercising)
expect ex-pect *expect*	We will **expect** you to come to our house. look for (expects expected expecting)
express ex-press *express*	Mary can **express herself** well. say what she wants to say (expresses expressed expressing) This is an **express** train. fast
eyes *eyes*	We see with our **eyes**. Mary's **eyes** are wide open. (eye)

I wash my hands and **face.**

We **face** the window.
look toward

(faces   faced   facing)

face
face

A **fact** is something that is true.
(facts)

fact
fact

Automobiles are made in a **factory.**
(factories)

factory
fac-to-ry
factory

The cloth will **fade.**
lose its color.

(fades   faded   fading)

fade
fade

The dog **failed**
was not able

to catch the cat.
(fail   fails   failing)

failed
failed

Bob is **fair** about his work.
honest

Mary divided her candy **fairly.**
evenly.

This is a **fair** day.
clear

People show and sell many things at the **fair.**

(fairs   fairer   fairest   fairly)

fair
fair

A B C D E **F** G H I J K L M N O P Q R S T U V W X Y Z

fairy
fair-y
fairy

See this **fairy!**

Fairies are make-believe people.

(fairies)

fall
fall

Humpty Dumpty sat on a wall.

Humpty Dumpty had a great **fall.**

Leaves **fall** from the trees
come down

in autumn.

(falls   fell   falling)

false
false

The story is **false.**
not true.

family
fam-i-ly
family

This is a **family.**

In this **family** there are

the father, mother, and two children.

(families)

fan
fan

This is an electric **fan.**

It helps you keep cool.

(fans)

far
far

Mary can throw the ball as **far** as Bob can.

Grandmother lives **far** away.
a long way off.

(farther   farthest)

The Eskimos live in a **faraway** / far off land.	**faraway** far-a-way *faraway*
The conductor on the train took our **fare.** / money for the ride. (fares)	**fare** *fare*
We went to a **farm** in the country. We saw horses and cows on the **farm.** (farms)	**farm** *farm*
This man is a **farmer.** He lives on a **farm.** He grows things to eat. (farmers)	**farmer** farm-er *farmer*
The farmer lives in the **farmhouse.** / house on the farm. (farmhouses)	**farmhouse** farm-house *farmhouse*
Mary runs slowly, but I can run **fast.** (faster fastest)	**fast** *fast*
Tom tried to **fasten** / lock the door. Mother **fastened** / buttoned Mary's dress. (fastens fastened fastening)	**fasten** fas-ten *fasten*

A B C D E F G H I J K L M N O P Q R S T U V W X Y Z

fat
fat

This man is **fat.**
not thin.

(fatter   fattest)

father
fa-ther
father

The woman is Jack's mother.
The man is Jack's **father.**
Father earns money
to care for his children.
(fathers)

fault
fault

Our teacher found **fault** with our work.
mistakes in

The accident was not anybody's **fault.**
No one made it happen.
(faults)

fear
fear

Mother has no **fear** of the dog.
is not afraid

(fears   feared   fearing)

feast
feast

The Pilgrims had a **feast**
many things to eat

on Thanksgiving.
(feasts   feasted   feasting)

feather
feath-er
feather

This is a **feather.**
Birds have **feathers.**
(feathers)

February
Feb-ru-ar-y
February

The second month of the year
is **February.**
February has 28 days.
Every four years **February** has 29 days.

See the girl **feed** the chickens. (feeds fed feeding)	**feed** *feed*	

See Bob **feel** / touch the elephant's trunk.
(feels felt feeling)

feel *feel*

Many bugs have **feelers.**
Bugs feel their way on the ground with their **feelers.**
(feeler)

feelers feel-ers *feelers*

The boy has bare **feet.**
Horses have four **feet.**
A **foot** is twelve inches long.
I am three **feet** tall.
(foot)

feet *feet*

The baby **fell** down.
She was not hurt.
(fall falls falling)

fell *fell*

Tom is a little **fellow.** / boy.
(fellows)

fellow fel-low *fellow*

Bob **felt** / touched the elephant's trunk.
(feel feels feeling)

felt *felt*

A B C D E F G H I J K L M N O P Q R S T U V W X Y Z

103

fence
fence

The **fence** is around the field.

The calf cannot
get over the **fence.**

(fences)

---

fender
fen-der
fender

The car has a bumped **fender.**

Fenders keep dirt
off the car.

(fenders)

---

fern
fern

This is a **fern** leaf.

Ferns have leaves
but no flowers.

(ferns)

---

few
few

Here are many flowers.

Here are | only a **few** | flowers.
| not many |

---

fiddle
fid-dle
fiddle

This is a | **fiddle.** |
| violin. |

Do you like the music
of a **fiddle?**

(fiddles)

---

field
field

The children play in the **field.**

Cows eat grass in the **field.**

(fields)

The lion is a | fierce | animal.
               | wild |

(fiercer   fiercest)

fierce
fierce

---

five   ten   **fifteen**
5   10   15

15

Can you count to **fifteen?**
Can you write the numbers from 1 to 15?

fifteen
fif-teen
fifteen

This is a whole pie cut into **five** pieces.

This is one **fifth,** or one of the five pieces.
(fifths)

fifth
fifth

---

thirty   forty   **fifty**
30   40   50

50

Fifty cents make one half-dollar.

fifty
fif-ty
fifty

Some boys | **fight.**
          | hit each other.

(fights   fought   fighting)

fight
fight

---

1   2   3   4   5   6   7   8   9   10
Each number is a **figure.**
Some cloth is plain.

This cloth has | **figures** | in it.
               | flowers or shapes |

(figures)

figure
fig-ure
figure

A
B
C
D
E
Ⓕ
G
H
I
J
K
L
M
N
O
P
Q
R
S
T
U
V
W
X
Y
Z

file
file

This is a nail **file.**

This **file** makes the fingernails smooth.

The children walked

in single **file.**
one line each behind the other.

(files   filed   filing)

---

fill
fill

Bob can **fill** his pail with sand.
make his pail full of

(fills   filled   filling)

---

finally
fi-nal-ly
finally

Finally the three bears came home.
At last

---

find
find

Little Bo-peep has lost her sheep,

And can't tell where to **find** them.
go get

(finds   found   finding)

---

fine
fine

Peter Rabbit said, "How **fine** I look!"

The man drove too fast.

He had to pay a **fine.**

Flour is **fine,** but oatmeal is coarse.

(fines   fined   fining)

---

finger
fin-ger
finger

I have five **fingers** on each hand.

Which **finger** is longest?

(fingers)

Jack is reading a book.

He will finish it soon. come to the end of

(finishes   finished   finishing)

finish
fin-ish
finish

The house is on **fire.**

It may burn down.
(fires)

fire
fire

This is a **fire alarm.**

We use it to call the firemen.
(fire alarms)

fire alarm
fire a-larm
fire alarm

We had **firecrackers** on the Fourth of July.

Did you ever set off a **firecracker?**
(firecrackers)

firecracker
fire-crack-er
firecracker

A **fire engine** is used
to throw water
on a fire.
(fire engines)

fire engine
fire en-gine
fire engine

The Indian sat by the **firelight.** light of the fire.

firelight
fire-light
firelight

The **fireman**
helped put out the fire.
(firemen)

fireman
fire-man
fireman

A B C D E **F** G H I J K L M N O P Q R S T U V W X Y Z

fireplace fire-place *fireplace*	They made a fire in the **fireplace.** (fireplaces)
fire station fire sta-tion *firestation*	Fire engines are kept at the **fire station.** (fire stations)
fire truck *fire truck*	The firemen drive the **fire truck.** The **fire truck** carries the ladder and hose. (fire trucks)
first *first*	Bob and Jane ran a race. Bob got to the tree **first.** before Jane did. Sunday is the **first** day of the week.
fish *fish*	Some **fish** are good to eat. **Fish** live in water. (fishes fished fishing)
fishhook fish-hook *fishhook*	We catch fish with a **fishhook.** (fishhooks)
fishline fish-line *fishline*	The **fishline** is tied to the pole. The **fishline** is a strong string. (fishlines)

My shoes are not too big or too small.

They just **fit** my feet.

       (fits   fitted   fitting)

fit

fit

Here are **five** stars.
5

Count them.

    (fifth   fifty)

5

five

five

See Father **fix** the tire.
mend

    (fixes   fixed   fixing)

fix

fix

This is an American **flag**.

    (flags)

flag

flag

These are snow**flakes**.

Each **flake** of snow is different.

    (flakes)

flake

flake

We saw the **flame** from the fire.
colored light

      (flames)

flame

flame

We paste the **flap**
   of the envelope.

We heard a noise.

It was a rope **flapping** against the house.
hitting

    (flaps   flapped   flapping)

flap

flap

A
B
C
D
E
(F)
G
H
I
J
K
L
M
N
O
P
Q
R
S
T
U
V
W
X
Y
Z

flash
flash

This is a **flash**light.

It **flashes.**
makes a light quickly.

(flashes   flashed   flashing)

---

flat
flat

The car has a **flat** tire.

Tables have **flat** tops.
even

(flatter   flattest)

---

flea
flea

The dog scratched his head.

A **flea** was biting him.
An insect

Fleas bite the dog to get his blood.
A **flea** does not have wings.

(fleas)

---

flew
flew

The bird **flew** away.

(fly   flies   flying)

---

flicker
flick-er
flicker

This bird is a **flicker.**
He is a kind of woodpecker.
He has yellowish wings.

(flickers)

---

float
float

The boat can **float.**
stay on top of the water.

(floats   floated   floating)

---

floor
floor

The children are sitting
on the **floor.**

(floors)

Bread is made from **flour.**
Flour is made of wheat.

flour
flour

See the water | **flow** / run | out of the pipe.

(flows   flowed   flowing)

flow
flow

Here are many **flowers.**   Here is one **flower.**

(flowers)

flower
flow-er
flower

The bird can **fly** high
into the sky.

This is a **fly.**

(flies   flew   flying)

fly
fly

Fold the paper to make a box.

(folds   folded   folding)

fold
fold

My dog likes to | **follow** me. / come after |

(follows   followed   following)

follow
fol-low
follow

Jane | is **fond** of / likes | the baby.

(fonder   fondest)

fond
fond

The things we eat
are **foods.**
We should eat
good **food.**

(foods)

food
food

A B C D E **F** G H I J K L M N O P Q R S T U V W X Y Z

foot
foot

The boy is standing on one **foot**.
Twelve inches make a **foot**.
We measure things with a **foot** ruler.
(feet)

footprints
foot-prints
footprints

We could see **footprints** in the sand.
marks of feet
(footprint)

for
for

I have a gift **for** Mother.

I know Bob is here **for** I saw him.
because

forehead
fore-head
forehead

Baby put her hand on her **forehead**.
(foreheads)

forest
forest

The land is covered with trees.
We call it a **forest.**
thick woods.
(forests)

forget
for-get
forget

I cannot buy an apple if I **forget**
do not remember

to bring my money.
(forgets   forgot   forgetting   forgotten)

forgive
for-give
forgive

Bob was a bad boy.

Mother said she would **forgive** him
not feel angry at

if he would promise to be good.
(forgives   forgave   forgiving   forgiven)

This is a **fork** to eat with.

The farmer uses a hay **fork** to pick up hay.
(forks)

| | **fork** |
| | *fork* |

The men built a fort to protect them strong building from their enemies.
(forts)

fort
fort

The soldier stepped forward. out in front. forth.

forward
for-ward
forward

The soldier fought the enemy. went to war against

Tom fought Bob. hit

(fight   fights   fighting)

fought
fought

Mary lost her pocketbook and Bob **found** it.
(find   finds   finding)

found
found

This is a **fountain** in the park.

We drink from a drinking **fountain**.
(fountains)

fountain
foun-tain
fountain

Here are four balls.
4

(fourth)

4

four
four

A B C D E F G H I J K L M N O P Q R S T U V W X Y Z

fox
fox

A fox looks something like a dog.
The **fox** has a bushy tail.

(foxes)

frame
frame

This is a **frame** for a picture.

This is a picture in a **frame.**

(frames)

frank
frank

The man was **frank** about the fight.
not afraid to talk

free
free

Bob set the dog **free.**
loose.

If you buy one pencil

you get another one **free.**
for nothing.

(freedom)

freezes
freez-es
freezes

Water **freezes** when it gets cold enough.
turns to ice

The rain **froze** on our window.

(freeze   froze   frozen   freezing   freezer)

fresh
fresh

The cake is **fresh.**
newly made.

The **fresh** air blew in the window.
cool

(fresher   freshest   freshly)

Monday, Tuesday, Wednesday, Thursday, and **Friday** are five days of the week. What are the other days?	**Friday** Fri-day *Friday*
Bob and Jack like each other. They are **friends**. Bob is Jack's **friend**. Jack is Bob's **friend**. (friends friendly)	**friend** *friend*
The dog ran toward the baby. It did not **frighten** her. / make her afraid. (frightens frightened frightening)	**frighten** fright-en *frighten*
The swing went to and **fro**. / backward and forward.	**fro** *fro*
The **frog** lives near the water. (frogs)	**frog** *frog*
The gingerbread boy ran away **from** the cow. I have a letter **from** Mother. The school is not far **from** here.	**from** *from*

A B C D E **F** G H I J K L M N O P Q R S T U V W X Y Z

115

front
front

The auto is in **front** of
before

the house.

Bob sits at the back of the room.
Mary sits at the **front**.

frost
frost

The **frost** on the window
frozen steam

made a picture.

The **frost** on the flowers
frozen dew

killed them.

fruit
fruit

Apple   Orange   Bananas   Peach

These are **fruits**.
We eat **fruit**.

(fruits)

fry
fry

Mother will **fry** the fish.
She will cook it in the skillet
on top of the stove.
(fries   fried   frying)

full
full

One box is empty.
The other is **full**.

fun
fun

We had **fun** playing in the water.
a nice time

116

Father told a **funny** story.
We laughed at the **funny** story.
    (funnier   funniest)

funny
fun-ny
funny

Mother has a **fur** coat.
The cat has a coat of **fur**.
    (furs)

fur
fur

We have a fire in the **furnace**.
The fire in the **furnace** keeps the house warm.
    (furnaces)

furnace
fur-nace
furnace

This is **furniture**.

furniture
fur-ni-ture
furniture

A B C D E (F) G H I J K L M N O P Q R S T U V W X Y Z

gain
gain

The boy did not | **gain** |
                | get |
anything

by telling what was not true.

(gains   gained   gaining)

gallop
gal-lop
gallop

See this horse **gallop.**

Gallop is one way a horse goes.

Galloping is something like jumping or leaping.

(gallops   galloped   galloping)

game
game

These boys are playing a **game.**

It is a ball **game.**

(games)

garage
ga-rage
garage

Father put the car into the **garage.**

(garages)

garden
gar-den
garden

The children are planting flowers and carrots in their **garden.**

(gardens)

gas
gas

Mother lights the **gas** in the stove.

The **gas** makes the fire.

This is a **gasoline** station.

Gasoline makes the auto go.

gasoline
gas-o-line
gasoline

The **gate** is closed.

(gates)

gate
gate

I will **gather** some flowers

pick

for Mother.

(gathers   gathered   gathering)

gather
gath-er
gather

Bob had seven apples
but he **gave** two to Mary.

(give   gives   giving   given)

gave
gave

The children were **gay.**

happy.

gay
gay

When the farmer wants his horse
to turn to the right, he says, "Gee."

gee
gee

Here are two **geese.**

Geese can swim.

(goose)

geese
geese

A
B
C
D
E
F
G
H
I
J
K
L
M
N
O
P
Q
R
S
T
U
V
W
X
Y
Z

A
B
C
D
E
F
G
H
I
J
K
L
M
N
O
P
Q
R
S
T
U
V
W
X
Y
Z

general
gen-er-al
general

Bob's father is a captain in the army.
Mary's father is a **general** in the army.
Both men are officers in the army.
They lead the other men.

(generals)

gentle
gen-tle
gentle

Our teacher has a **gentle** voice.
soft
kind

(gently)

gentleman
gen-tle-man
gentleman

A **gentleman** is a man who is kind and polite.

(gentlemen)

get
get

Jack and Jill went up the hill
To **get** a pail of water.

(gets   got   getting   gotten)

giant
gi-ant
giant

This man is a **giant**.
A **giant** is large and strong.

(giants)

gift
gift

Today is my birthday.

Mother gave me a nice **gift.**
present.

(gifts)

gingerbread
gin-ger-bread
gingerbread

I like **gingerbread.**
cake with ginger in it.

This is a **gingerbread** boy
Mother made for me.

See how long this **giraffe's** neck and legs are. He has spots on his body. He can eat from tall trees. (giraffes)	**giraffe** gi-raffe *giraffe*
This **girl** is Mary. (girls)	**girl** *girl*
I have two apples. I will **give** you one. make you a gift of (gives gave giving given)	**give** *give*
Mary went to the party. Bob said, "I am **glad** that you came." happy (gladly)	**glad** *glad*
Every time the fire engine goes by, I **glance** out the window. look quickly (glances glanced glancing)	**glance** *glance*
Windows are made of **glass**. Some dishes are made of **glass**. This is a **glass** with milk in it. (glasses)	**glass** *glass*

A
B
C
D
E
F
(G)
H
I
J
K
L
M
N
O
P
Q
R
S
T
U
V
W
X
Y
Z

glossy
glos-sy
glossy

Bob rubbed his shoes
until they were **glossy.**
smooth and shiny.

---

glove
glove

This is a woolen **glove.**

Two gloves make
a pair of **gloves.**
(gloves)

---

glue
glue

Mary broke her doll.

Father **glued** it together for her.
stuck

Glue is sticky.

It holds things together.
(glues   glued   gluing)

---

go
go

Father has an auto.

We will **go** for a ride.
(goes   gone   going)

---

goat
goat

This is a **goat.**

Some people drink **goat's** milk.
(goats)

---

gobble
gob-ble
gobble

The duck says, "Quack, quack."

The turkey says, **"Gobble, gobble."**

Some children **gobble** their food.
eat their food fast.

(gobbles   gobbled   gobbling)

Mother took Baby for a ride in the **go-cart.** (go-carts)	**go-cart** go-cart *go-cart*
God made the world. **God** is ruler of the world.	**God** *God*
These things are made of **gold.** **Gold** is a yellow metal. (golden)	**gold** *gold*
This yellow flower is the **goldenrod.** It grows in fields and by the roadside.	**goldenrod** gold-en-rod *goldenrod*
There are two **goldfish** in the bowl.	**goldfish** gold-fish *goldfish*
A golf club A golf bag A golf ball Father plays **golf.**	**golf** *golf*
Father has **gone** to work. (go goes going)	**gone** *gone*

good
good

Tom is a **good** boy.
not a bad

good-by
good-by
good-by

The children said **good-by** to their mother.

good morning
good morn-ing
good morning

Mary says **good morning** to her mother when she gets up in the morning.

good night
good night

Mary says **good night** to her mother when she goes to bed at night.

goose
goose

This is a **goose.**

A **goose** is good to eat.

A **goose** can swim.

(geese)

got
got

We **got** good marks at school.

Father **got** a new hat.

(get   gets   getting   gotten)

gown
gown

A **gown** is a dress.

This is Mother's evening **gown.**

(gowns)

Mary is a graceful dancer.
beautiful

(gracefully)

graceful
grace-ful
graceful

I go to school.

I am in the first grade.
class.

(grades)

grade
grade

A potato is a vegetable.

Wheat is a **grain.**

Corn is a **grain,** too.

(grains)

grain
grain

Your father's father
is your **grandfather.**

Your mother's father
is your **grandfather,** too.

(grandfathers)

grandfather
grand-fa-ther
grandfather

I call my grandmother **Grandma.**

(grandmas)

grandma
grand-ma
grandma

Your father's mother
is your **grandmother.**

Your mother's mother
is your **grandmother,** too.

(grandmothers)

grandmother
grand-moth-er
grandmother

A
B
C
D
E
F
G
H
I
J
K
L
M
N
O
P
Q
R
S
T
U
V
W
X
Y
Z

grandpa
grand-pa
grandpa

I call my grandfather **Grandpa.**
(grandpas)

grant
grant

The fairy would not | **grant** | the woodcutter
give

his wish.
(grants   granted   granting)

grapes
grapes

This is a bunch of **grapes.**

Grapes are red, purple, or green.

Did you ever eat **grapes?**
(grape)

grapevine
grape-vine
grapevine

Berries grow on a bush.

Cherries grow on a tree.

Grapes grow on a vine.

We call it a **grapevine.**
(grapevines)

grass
grass

Green **grass** grows in the yard.

Cows eat **grass.**
(grasses   grassy)

grasshopper
grass-hop-per
grasshopper

The **grasshopper** hops.

See how long his legs are.

Grasshoppers eat the things farmers grow.

Farmers do not like **grasshoppers.**
(grasshoppers)

Gravel is small stones. Some roads are made of **gravel.**	**gravel** grav-el *gravel*
Some mice are white and some are **gray.**	**gray** *gray*
Mother gave a party for me. It was a ⎡**great**⎤ surprise. ⎣big⎦ George Washington was a **great** man. He did many good things for his country. (greater greatest)	**great** *great*
Two dogs were eating. The bigger dog ⎡was **greedy.**⎤ ⎣wanted more than his share.⎦ (greedier greediest)	**greedy** greed-y *greedy*
Grass is **green.** When the traffic light is **green,** the children cross the street.	**green** *green*
The flowers **grew** in the garden. (grow grows growing grown)	**grew** *grew*
The **grocer** sells us food. (grocers)	**grocer** gro-cer *grocer*

A B C D E F G H I J K L M N O P Q R S T U V W X Y Z

grocery gro-cer-y *grocery*	We buy crackers, sugar, and other things to eat at the **grocery** store. (groceries)
groceryman gro-cer-y-man *groceryman*	The man who runs the grocery store is called the **groceryman.** (grocerymen)
ground *ground*	We put the seeds into the **ground.** Mother **ground** the coffee. (grind grinds grinding)
group *group*	This is one boy. This is a **group** of boys. number (groups)
grow *grow*	Rain makes the flowers **grow.** become larger. (grows grew growing grown)
growl *growl*	The dog is cross. I heard him **growl** at us. (growls growled growling)
grown-up grown-up *grownup*	Jack is a **grown-up** boy now. He will get no taller.

The Billy Goat has a **gruff** / deep voice.

gruff
gruff

The dog will **guard** / watch over the baby.

(guards   guarded   guarding)

guard
guard

Bob had some apples in a box.

I tried to **guess** how many there were.

(guesses   guessed   guessing)

guess
guess

We had a **guest** / company for dinner.

(guests)

guest
guest

Bob will **guide** you / show you the way to the zoo.

(guides   guided   guiding)

guide
guide

The children do not chew **gum** in school.
It is not polite.

gum
gum

A gun

Men shoot with a **gun.**

(guns)

gun
gun

A B C D E F (G) H I J K L M N O P Q R S T U V W X Y Z

had
had

Bob asked Mother for some milk.

She gave him all she **had.**

(have   has   having)

hair
hair

Mary is combing her **hair.**

(hairs   hairy)

half
half

The apple is cut into two pieces.

Each piece is a **half.**

(halves)

hall
hall

John put his coat in the **hall.**

There is a **hall** between the bedroom
and the bathroom.

(halls)

Halloween
Hal-low-een
Halloween

The children are having
a **Halloween** party.

See their jack-o'-lantern.

Halloween is the last day of October.

ham
ham

This meat is **ham.**

We get **ham** from pigs.

(hams)

hammer
ham-mer
hammer

This is a **hammer.**

We pound with a **hammer.**

(hammers   hammered   hammering)

See Mary's **hand.**		**hand** *hand*
We have two **hands.** (hands)		
A clean handkerchief (handkerchiefs)		**handkerchief** hand-ker-chief *handkerchief*
The cup has a broken **handle.** (handles handled handling)		**handle** han-dle *handle*
The baby is very **handsome.** good looking.		**handsome** hand-some *handsome*
I like to **hang** clothes on the clothesline. My hat **hangs** on a hook. (hangs hanging hung)		**hang** *hang*
They put the airplane in the **hangar.** (hangars)		**hangar** hang-ar *hangar*
Cross the street with the green light, or something may **happen.** take place. What **happened to** my ball? became of (happens happened happening)		**happen** hap-pen *happen*

A B C D E F G (H) I J K L M N O P Q R S T U V W X Y Z

happy hap-py *happy*	John is a good boy. This makes Mother feel **happy.** / joyful. (happiness happily happier happiest)
hard *hard*	Fur is soft. Stones are **hard.** (harder hardest)
hare *hare*	This is a **hare.** He looks like a rabbit but he is larger. (hares)
harm *harm*	This dog will not **harm** / hurt you. (harms harmed harming harmful)
has *has*	I have a big doll and Betty **has** a small one. (have had having)
hatch *hatch*	The hen is sitting on the eggs. In three weeks chicks will **hatch** from / come out of the eggs. (hatches hatched hatching)
hate *hate*	The rats **hate** / do not like the cat. (hates hated hating)

John and Mary have **hats** on their heads. (hat)		**hats** *hats*

Give me all the money you **have.**
                 own.
 	
   (has   had   having)
		have
		have

Bob and Mary have some apples but we **haven't** any. do not have		**haven't** *haven't*
This bird is a **hawk.** He eats chickens. (hawks)		**hawk** *hawk*
Hay is dried grass. Cows eat **hay.**		**hay** *hay*
See the boy run. **He** runs fast. **He** is home. Father		**he** *he*
Father has his hat on his **head.** (heads)		**head** *head*
Mother called to Bob but he did not **hear** her. We **hear** with our ears. (hears heard hearing)		**hear** *hear*

A
B
C
D
E
F
G
(H)
I
J
K
L
M
N
O
P
Q
R
S
T
U
V
W
X
Y
Z

A
B
C
D
E
F
G
(H)
I
J
K
L
M
N
O
P
Q
R
S
T
U
V
W
X
Y
Z

heard *heard*	Mother called Bob again.
	He **heard** her that time.
	(hear hears hearing)

heart *heart*	This valentine is shaped like a **heart.**
	The doctor listened to the beating of my **heart.**
	(hearts)

heat *heat*	The fire will **heat** / warm the soup.
	The **heat** / hot weather made the horse tired.
	(heats heated heating)

heavy heav-y *heavy*	Mary could not carry the big chair.
	It was too **heavy.**
	(heavier heaviest)

| **heel** *heel* | A heel on a shoe   A person's heel |
| | (heels) |

| **held** *held* | The baby cried, so Mother **held** her in her arms. |
| | (hold   holds   holding) |

| **hello** hel-lo *hello* | When I meet the children I say **hello** to them. |

Jane tried to lift the chair.
Bob said, "I will **help** you."
(helps   helped   helping   helper   helpers)

help
help

Have you heard about the little red **hen?**
(hens)

hen
hen

The hen lives in a **henhouse.**
(henhouses)

henhouse
hen-house
henhouse

The girl has the doll in **her** arms.

her
her

Jack asked where the cookies were.
Mother said, "Here."
"In this place."

here
here

The little girl can dress all by **herself.**

herself
her-self
herself

Jack **hid** his ball in the box
so that the baby would not find it.
(hide   hides   hiding   hidden)

hid
hid

Jack said, "Shut your eyes while **I hide** the ball."
(hides   hiding   hidden   hid)

hide
hide

The children play **hide-and-seek.**

hide-and-seek
hide-and-seek
hide-and-seek

A B C D E F G (H) I J K L M N O P Q R S T U V W X Y Z

high *high*	The bird flew **high** up in the sky. (higher highest)
hill *hill*	Jack and Jill went up the **hill.** (hills)
him *him*	Bob asked me for some pennies. I gave **him** all I had.
himself him-self *himself*	The little boy can dress **himself.**
his *his*	The boy plays with **his** dog. / the dog he owns.
hit *hit*	The boy will **hit** the ball with the bat. (hits hitting)
hive *hive*	This is a bee's **hive.** / house. Bees live in the hive. (hives)
hold *hold*	Mother likes to **hold** the baby in her arms. (holds held holding)

Mother carries hot pans with a **holder**. (holders)	**holder** hold-er *holder*
There is a **hole** in the window. (holes)	**hole** *hole*
The owl lives in	**hollow**
in | a **hollow** | tree. | an empty |	hol-low *hollow*
Father goes to work in the morning. He comes | **home** | at night. | to the house where we live | (homes)	**home** *home*
An **honest** man tells the truth. He does not steal or cheat.	**honest** hon-est *honest*
Bees make **honey** from the juice they get from flowers. It is sweet and good to eat.	**honey** hon-ey *honey*
Hear the | **honk** | of the auto horn! | noise | (honks honked honking)	**honk** *honk*
Little Red Riding **Hood** wore a **hood** on her head. (hoods)	**hood** *hood*

A
B
C
D
E
F
G
(H)
I
J
K
L
M
N
O
P
Q
R
S
T
U
V
W
X
Y
Z

hook
hook

The man hung his coat on the **hook.**
(hooks)

hoop
hoop

Bob is rolling a **hoop.**
(hoops)

hop
hop

See these boys **hop** on one foot.

Can you **hop?**
(hops   hopped   hopping)

horn
horn

This is a **horn** to blow.

The goat has **horns** on his head.
(horns)

horse
horse

Grandfather rides a **horse.**

He let Bob ride on the **horse's** back.
(horses)

horse chestnut
horse chest-nut
horse chestnut

This tree is a **horse chestnut.**

It has very big leaves.

The seed is a big brown nut.
(horse chestnuts)

Horse chestnut tree   Leaves   Seeds

These are | **hose.** |
| **stockings.** |

We use a garden **hose**
to water the garden.
(hoses)

When Father was sick, he went to the **hospital.**

The nurse took care of Father
while he was in the **hospital.**
(hospitals)

In summer the sun makes us | **hot.** |
| **very warm.** |

(hotter   hottest)

When Mary went to the city,
she stayed in a **hotel.**

The **hotel** has many rooms.

She ate and slept in the **hotel.**
(hotels)

From 8 o'clock until 9 o'clock
is one **hour.**

One **hour** is sixty minutes.
There are 24 **hours** in a day.
(hours)

A B C D E F G (H) I J K L M N O P Q R S T U V W X Y Z

139

house
house

People live in **houses.**

This **house** is made of wood.

(houses)

how
how

The girl has two books.

How many have you?

Do you know **how** to count to a hundred?

however
how-ev-er
however

There are no apples.

However, you may have some strawberries.

hug
hug

See Mary **hug** the baby.
put her arms around

(hugs   hugged   hugging)

huge
huge

A **huge** tree
very large

grew by the door.

hump
hump

This camel has one **hump**
on his back.

This camel has two **humps**
on his back.

(humps)

140

Can you count to one **hundred?** 100?

(hundreds)

100

hundred
hun-dred
hundred

Mother **hung** clothes on the line.

(hang   hangs   hanging)

hung
hung

Please give me something to eat.

I am so **hungry.**

(hungrier   hungriest)

hungry
hun-gry
hungry

Father went into the woods to **hunt** / look for rabbits.

I lost my hat.

Will you help me **hunt** / look for it?

(hunts   hunted   hunting   hunter   hunters)

hunt
hunt

The children cheered the flag.

They said, **"Hurrah! Hurrah!"**

hurrah
hur-rah
hurrah

The fire bell is ringing.

We must **hurry.** / move fast.

(hurries   hurried   hurrying)

hurry
hur-ry
hurry

I cut my hands.

They **hurt** / pain me.

(hurts   hurting)

hurt
hurt

A
B
C
D
E
F
G
Ⓗ
I
J
K
L
M
N
O
P
Q
R
S
T
U
V
W
X
Y
Z

husband hus-band *husband*	Father is my mother's **husband.** Mother is the wife. (husbands)
hush *hush*	The baby is asleep. **Hush!** You may wake her. Be still! (hushes hushed hushing)
husk *husk*	This ear of corn has the **husk** on it. This is the **husk** covering without the corn. (husks husked husking)
hut *hut*	The hunter lives in this old **hut.** little house. (huts)
hydrant hy-drant *hydrant*	Do not park near the fire **hydrant.** The firemen could not get to the **hydrant** for water if there were a fire. (hydrants)

Jack has a cat but **I** have a dog.

I
I

I like to skate on **ice**
in the winter.

(icy)

ice
ice

This is an **iceberg.**
It is like a large floating
island of ice in the ocean.

(icebergs)

iceberg
ice-berg
iceberg

Do you like **ice cream** in a cone?

ice cream
ice cream

I have an **idea** that my rabbit is lost.
think

(ideas)

idea
i-de-a
idea

Father went to see **if** the postman had gone.
whether

if
if

The Eskimos live in an **igloo.**
It is made of hard snow.
(igloos)

igloo
ig-loo
igloo

I am **ill** today.
sick

ill
ill

A
B
C
D
E
F
G
H
(I)
J
K
L
M
N
O
P
Q
R
S
T
U
V
W
X
Y
Z

I'll
I'll

"**I'll** get the goats out of the turnip patch,"
"I will

said the bee.

I'm
I'm

I'm a big boy.
I am

impolite
im-po-lite
impolite

Bob was **impolite** to his sister.
not polite

He used very bad **manners**.

in
in

Where is the cat?
She is **in** her bed.

inch
inch

This line is one **inch** long. ———
Twelve **inches** make a foot.

(inches)

increase
in-crease
increase

If you blow air into the balloon,
it will **increase** in size.
become larger.

(increases   increased   increasing)

indeed
in-deed
indeed

Simple Simon met a pieman
Going to the fair.
Said Simple Simon to the pieman,
"Let me taste your ware."
Said the pieman to Simple Simon,
"Show me first your penny."
Said Simple Simon to the pieman,

"**Indeed** I haven't any."
"Truthfully

See this **Indian.** His hat is made of feathers. **Indians** lived in America before the white people came. (Indians)	**Indian** In-di-an *Indian*
Mary spilled **ink** on her paper.	**ink** *ink*
The bee is an **insect.** Flies are **insects,** too. (insects)	**insect** in-sect *insect*
Where is the hen? The hen is **inside** the henhouse. not outside	**inside** in-side *inside*
Mary will go **instead** of Bob. in the place	**instead** in-stead *instead*
The children were **interested** in the story. They wanted to hear all of it. (interest interests interesting)	**interested** in-ter-est-ed *interested*
Bob went **into** the house.	**into** in-to *into*

A
B
C
D
E
F
G
H
Ⓘ
J
K
L
M
N
O
P
Q
R
S
T
U
V
W
X
Y
Z

invite
in-vite
invite

We are having a party.

We will **invite** teacher to come.
ask

(invites   invited   inviting   invitation)

---

iris
i-ris
iris

This flower is an **iris.**
Irises are of many colors.
(irises)

---

iron
i-ron
iron

This is an electric **iron.**

Mother will **iron** the clothes.
Many tools are made of **iron.**
(irons   ironed   ironing)

---

ironing board
i-ron-ing board
ironing board

This is an **ironing board.**
Mother irons the clothes
on an **ironing board.**
(ironing boards)

---

is
is

Bob **is** playing.
This **is** a nice day.

---

island
is-land
island

This land is an **island.**
It has water
all around it.
(islands)

---

isn't
isn't

This **isn't** my birthday.
is not

146

	it
Mary has a doll. Father gave **it** to her.	*it*

	it's
[It's] raining today. [It is]	*it's*

	itself
The barn stood in the field all [by **itself.** alone.]	it-self *itself*

	I've
[I've] a box of toys. [I have]	*I've*

A
B
C
D
E
F
G
H
Ⓘ
J
K
L
M
N
O
P
Q
R
S
T
U
V
W
X
Y
Z

A
B
C
D
E
F
G
H
I
(J)
K
L
M
N
O
P
Q
R
S
T
U
V
W
X
Y
Z

jacket
jack-et
jacket

Father is wearing a **jacket.**
short coat.

(jackets)

jack-in-the-pulpit
jack-in-the-pul-pit
jack-in-the-pulpit

This flower is called
a **jack-in-the-pulpit.**
(jack-in-the-pulpits)

jack-o'-lantern
jack-o'-lan-tern
jack-o'-lantern

The children made
this **jack-o'-lantern.**
(jack-o'-lanterns)

jail
jail

People who do not obey the law are put in **jail.**
(jails)

jam
jam

Most boys and girls like to eat raspberry **jam**
on their bread.

It is made of berries and sugar.

janitor
jan-i-tor
janitor

The man who keeps the school clean
is the **janitor.**

(janitors)

January
Jan-u-ar-y
January

January is the first month
of the year.

New Year's Day is in **January.**

jars
jars

Mother cans fruit in glass **jars.**
(jar)

I like **jelly** on my bread.

Grape **jelly** is made from sugar and grape juice.

jelly
jel-ly
jelly

Jack had fun.

He told Jane a | **joke.**
| funny story.

(jokes   joked   joking   joker)

joke
joke

Bob is very | **jolly.**
| full of fun.

(jollier   jolliest)

jolly
jol-ly
jolly

This flower is a **jonquil.**

It is yellow.

It blossoms in spring.

(jonquils)

jonquil
jon-quil
jonquil

Mary and her father

are going on a long | **journey**
| trip

to the country.

(journeys)

journey
jour-ney
journey

The gifts brought | **joy**
| happiness

to the sick children.

(joyful   joyfully   joyous)

joy
joy

The teacher will | **judge** our work.
| see if our work is good.

(judges   judged   judging)

judge
judge

A
B
C
D
E
F
G
H
I
Ⓙ
K
L
M
N
O
P
Q
R
S
T
U
V
W
X
Y
Z

juice
juice

Mother is squeezing the **juice** out of the orange.

We like orange **juice.**

(juices   juicy   juicier   juiciest)

July
Ju-ly
July

July is the seventh month of the year.
We have a parade
on the Fourth of **July.**

---

jump
jump

The boy can **jump** the rope.
(jumps   jumped   jumping)

June
June

June is the sixth month of the year.
School is out in May or **June.**

---

jungle
jun-gle
jungle

The tiger is in the **jungle.**
(jungles)

---

just
just

Father **just** came.
came a short time ago.

The party was **just** fine.
very

Father gave me a rabbit to **keep.**
have always.

I **keep** it in a box.
have

(keeps   kept   keeping   keeper)

keep
keep

Father gave me a rabbit.

When it was sick, I **kept** it in the house.

(keep   keeps   keeping   keeper)

kept
kept

This is an ear of corn.

This is a **kernel** of corn.
seed

This is a walnut.

This is the **kernel** of the walnut.

(kernels)

kernel
ker-nel
kernel

A tea kettle   We cook in this **kettle.**
We boil water in a tea **kettle.**

(kettles)

kettle
ket-tle
kettle

This is a **key.**

We lock our door with a **key.**

(keys)

key
key

A
B
C
D
E
F
G
H
I
J
(K)
L
M
N
O
P
Q
R
S
T
U
V
W
X
Y
Z

khaki
kha-ki
khaki

The soldier's clothes are made of **khaki** cloth.

kick
kick

See Tom **kick** the ball with his foot.
(kicks   kicked   kicking)

kid
kid

Mother wears **kid** gloves.

They are made of leather.

A **kid** is a baby goat.

killed
killed

The hunter | **killed** the wolf.
put the wolf to death.

(kills   kill   killing)

kimono
ki-mo-no
kimono

This is a **kimono**.

It is a loose dress.

Some women wear **kimonos** in the house.
(kimonos)

kind
kind

What **kind** of ice cream do you like?

Mother is **kind** to her children.
does nice things for

(kinds   kinder   kindest   kindly)

kindergarten
kin-der-gar-ten
kindergarten

I go to school.

I am in the first grade.

Last year I was in the **kindergarten**.

We learn to work together in the **kindergarten**.
(kindergartens)

This man is a **king.** He is something like our president. He is a ruler. (kings)	**king** *king*
The land which a king rules is a **kingdom.** (kingdoms)	**kingdom** king-dom *kingdom*
See Tom **kiss** the baby's cheek. (kisses kissed kissing)	**kiss** *kiss*
This is a **kitchen.** Mother cooks in the **kitchen.** (kitchens)	**kitchen** kitch-en *kitchen*
This **kite** has a tail and a string. (kites)	**kite** *kite*
The baby cat is called a **kitten.** (kittens)	**kitten** kit-ten *kitten*
Jane calls her pet kitten **"Kitty."** (kitties)	**kitty** kit-ty *kitty*
Bob fell and hurt his **knee.** (knees)	**knee** *knee*

A B C D E F G H I J Ⓚ L M N O P Q R S T U V W X Y Z

kneeling
kneel-ing
kneeling

This boy is **kneeling.**
standing on his knees.

(kneel   kneels   knelt)

knew
knew

Mary read her story.

She **knew** all the words.
(know   knows   knowing   known)

knife
knife

This is a table **knife.**

We cut with a **knife.**

(knives)

knock
knock

I saw a small girl **knock**
rap

on the door.
(knocks   knocked   knocking)

know
know

There was an old woman
Who lived in a shoe.
She had so many children
She didn't **know** what to do.
(knows   knew   knowing   known)

knowledge
knowl-edge
knowledge

The old man understands
many things.

He has much **knowledge.**

This is lace for a dress.

This is a shoe**lace.**
string.

The boy **laces** his shoes
with a shoe**lace.**
(laces   laced   lacing)

lace
lace

This is a small **lad.**
boy.

(lads   laddie)

lad
lad

Father uses a **ladder**
when he paints the house.
(ladders)

ladder
lad-der
ladder

A **lady** is a woman who is kind and polite.
(ladies)

lady
la-dy
lady

This water is a **lake.**
There is land all around it.
(lakes)

lake
lake

A baby sheep is called a **lamb.**
(lambs)

lamb
lamb

A little lamb is sometimes called a **lambkin.**
(lambkins)

lambkin
lamb-kin
lambkin

A B C D E F G H I J K L M N O P Q R S T U V W X Y Z

155

A
B
C
D
E
F
G
H
I
J
K
(L)
M
N
O
P
Q
R
S
T
U
V
W
X
Y
Z

lamps
lamps

These are **lamps.**

They make light for us at night.

(lamp)

land
land

Boats sail on the water.

Autos run on the | **land.**
ground. |

(lands   landed   landing)

language
lan-guage
language

I speak the English **language.**

What **language** do you speak?

(languages)

lantern
lan-tern
lantern

These are **lanterns.**

Lanterns make light.

The farmer carries the **lantern** to the barn.

(lanterns)

lap
lap

Mother held the baby in her **lap.**

(laps)

lard
lard

Lard is a fat.

It comes from pigs.

Lard is sometimes used for cooking.

The elephant is not small.

He is | **large.**
       | big. |

(larger   largest)

large
large

This bird is a meadow **lark.**

He makes his nest on the ground.

He sings a pretty song.

(larks)

lark
lark

This is a **larva.**

Some **larvae** are called caterpillars.

(larvae)

larva
lar-va
larva

Bob is first in the line.

Jane is **last** in the line.

How long did the show | **last?**
                      | go on? |

It **lasted** one hour.

(lasts   lasted   lasting)

last
last

Tom came to school early,

but Mary came | **late.**
              | after time. |

(later   latest)

late
late

Tom told a funny story.

See Bob **laugh** at it.

(laughs   laughed   laughing)

laugh
laugh

A
B
C
D
E
F
G
H
I
J
K
Ⓛ
M
N
O
P
Q
R
S
T
U
V
W
X
Y
Z

A
B
C
D
E
F
G
H
I
J
K
L
M
N
O
P
Q
R
S
T
U
V
W
X
Y
Z

law
law

A **law** tells what to do.

We should all obey the | **laws** / rules |

made for our country.

(laws)

lawn
lawn

Father is mowing the **lawn.**

(lawns)

lay
lay

See Mother | **lay** / place | the baby on the bed.

The hen **laid** an egg.

(lays   laid   laying)

lazy
la-zy
lazy

Some people | are **lazy.** / will not work. |

(lazier   laziest)

lead
lead

The children are playing a game.

Bob wanted to | **lead.** / show them how. |

He wanted to be the **leader.**

(leads   led   leading   leader)

lead
lead

This is a **lead** pencil.

We write with a **lead** pencil. *Mary*

leaf
leaf

These are **leaves** from trees.

A maple leaf   An oak leaf

(leaves)

Jack Spratt would eat no fat.
His wife would eat no **lean**.
And so between them, you see,
They kept the platter clean.

The ladder | **leans** |
        | rests |

against the house.
(leans   leaned   leaning)

lean
lean

A frog can | **leap** | high.
        | jump |

(leaps   leaped   leaping)

leap
leap

In school we | **learn** | to read.
        | find out how |

(learns   learned   learning)

learn
learn

Shoes are made of **leather**.

Belts are made of **leather**.

Pocketbooks are made of **leather**.

leather
leath-er
leather

Mary had to | **leave** | the party before we did.
        | go away from |

(leaves   leaving   left)

leave
leave

The boy **led** the pony to the barn.
(lead   leads   leading)

led
led

A B C D E F G H I J K **L** M N O P Q R S T U V W X Y Z

left
left

Bob writes with his **left** hand.

We **left** the party early.
went away from

Mary has one apple **left**.

---

legs
legs

We stand on our **legs**.

We have two **legs**.

Dogs and horses have four **legs**.

The table has four **legs**.
(leg)

---

lemon
lem-on
lemon

This is a **lemon**.

Lemons are yellow and sour.
(lemons)

---

lemonade
lem-on-ade
lemonade

Lemonade is made of lemon juice, sugar, and water.

Lemonade is good to drink.

---

length
length

My ruler is twelve inches in **length**.
long.

---

less
less

I have **less** money than you.

I do not have as much money as you.
(little   least)

---

let
let

Be good and Mother will **let** you play.
allow you to

Let's sing a song.
Let us

let's
lets

A B C   These are **letters**.

Do you know all the A B C's?

I will send this **letter**
through the mail.
(letters)

letter
let-ter
letter

This is a head of **lettuce**.
It looks like cabbage.

lettuce
let-tuce
lettuce

This is a **library**.

We get books from the **library**.
(libraries)

library
li-brar-y
library

See the dog **lick** Mary's hand.
(licks   licked   licking)

lick
lick

Mother puts a **lid** on the kettle
cover

when she cooks.
(lids)

lid
lid

I am sleepy.

I will **lie** on the bed and sleep.

George Washington said, "I cannot tell a **lie**."
(lies   lay   lain   lying)

lie
lie

A
B
C
D
E
F
G
H
I
J
K
Ⓛ
M
N
O
P
Q
R
S
T
U
V
W
X
Y
Z

life
life

Tom read about the **life** of George Washington.

(lives)

---

lift
lift

The man was strong.

He could **lift** the heavy box.
raise

(lifts   lifted   lifting)

---

light
light

One box was heavy but the other was **light.**

It is dark at night but it is **light** in the daytime.

This is an electric **light.**

(lights   lighted   lighting   lit)
(lighter   lightest   lightly)

---

like
like

Mary's dress is **like** Jane's.
the same as

I **like** milk.
enjoy

(likes   liked   liking)

---

lily
lil-y
lily

This flower is a **lily.**

It grows from a bulb, not a seed.

(lilies)

---

limb
limb

The boy climbed out

on the **limb** of the tree.
branch

Legs and arms are called **limbs.**

(limbs)

This man is Abraham **Lincoln.**
He was a president of the United States.

Lincoln
Lin-coln
Lincoln

A straight line   A fish line   A clothesline
There are many kinds of **lines.**
Here are three kinds.
(lines)

line
line

This is a **lion.**
He is wild.
He lives in a jungle.
(lions)

lion
li-on
lion

Father's pipe is between his **lips.**
(lip)

lips
lips

Mary wrote a **list** of names on her paper.
     many
(lists   listed   listing)

list
list

Mother wanted to hear the music.
She sat down to **listen** to the music on the radio.
(listens   listened   listening)

listen
lis-ten
listen

One doll is big
but the other is **little.**
     small.
(littler   littlest)

little
lit-tle
little

A
B
C
D
E
F
G
H
I
J
K
(L)
M
N
O
P
Q
R
S
T
U
V
W
X
Y
Z

live
live

The old woman **lived** in a shoe.

I **live** in a house.

(lives   lived   living)

load
load

This is a **load** of hay.
wagon filled with

The men **load** the wagon with hay.
fill

(loads   loaded   loading)

loaf
loaf

This is a **loaf** of bread.

We slice off pieces of a **loaf.**

Mother makes meat **loaf** sometimes.

(loaves)

lock
lock

This is a **lock.**

Father will **lock** the auto door with a key.
fasten

(locks   locked   locking)

log
log

The frog is sitting

on a **log.**
part of a tree trunk.

(logs)

long
long

This pencil is short.

This pencil is **long.**

(longer   longest)

Father lost his hat.

I will **look** for it.
try to find

Look at my new shoes.
See

(looks   looked   looking)

look
look

Jack can see himself

in the **looking glass.**
mirror.

(looking glasses)

looking glass
look-ing glass
looking glass

The dog's collar is **loose.**
not tight.

The dog is **loose.**
not tied up.

(looser   loosest   loosely   loosen)

loose
loose

Little Bo Peep has **lost** her sheep,
And can't tell where to find them.
Leave them alone, and they'll come home,
Wagging their tails behind them.

(lose   loses   losing)

lost
lost

Bob had a **lot** of marbles.
great many

Father built a house on his **lot.**
piece of land.

(lots)

lot
lot

Mother dropped a pan.
It made a **loud** noise.

(louder   loudest   loudly)

loud
loud

A
B
C
D
E
F
G
H
I
J
K
Ⓛ
M
N
O
P
Q
R
S
T
U
V
W
X
Y
Z

loves
loves

Mother **loves** her baby.
| is very fond of |

(love   loved   loving)
(lovely   lovelier   loveliest)
(lovers)

low
low

One airplane is high in the sky.

The other one is **low.**
(lower   lowest)

lullaby
lull-a-by
lullaby

Mother sang a **lullaby** to the baby.
| soft song |

(lullabies)

lump
lump

Tom fell down and hit his head.

It made a big **lump.**

Father put a big **lump** of coal
| piece |

on the fire.
(lumps)

lunch
lunch

I eat my **lunch** when I go home at noon.

We do not eat as much for **lunch**
as we do for dinner.
(lunches)

	machine
A sewing machine A washing machine A machine in a factory These are **machines.** **Machines** make work easy. (machines)	**machine** ma-chine *machine*

The man was **mad.**
              crazy.
 	
The dog is **mad.**
           sick and may bite.
 	
    (madder   maddest)
	mad
	mad

Tom wanted a kite. Grandfather **made** a kite for him. (make makes making)	**made** *made*

The fairy waved her **magic** wand,
    and three rabbits hopped out of the basket.
      (magical)
	magic
	mag-ic
	magic

A girl is sometimes called a **maid.**
Grandmother has a **maid** to do her work.
              girl
      (maids)
	maid
	maid

A B C D E F G H I J K L (M) N O P Q R S T U V W X Y Z

maiden
maid-en
maiden

A girl is sometimes called
a maid or a **maiden.**
(maidens)

mail
mail

This is a **mailbox.**

Mary put the **mail**
letters and packages

in the **mail**box.
(mails   mailed   mailing)

mailbag
mail-bag
mailbag

The postman

carries a **mailbag.**
bag for letters.

(mailbags)

main
main

The **main** street in our town is Second Street.
largest

The **main** thing to do is to listen
most important

when someone else is talking.

maize
maize

This corn is sometimes called **maize.**

Mother wants a birdhouse.

I will **make** it for her.

   (makes   made   making)

make
make

Did you see my | **mamma?**
               | mother?

      (mammas)

mamma
mam-ma
mamma

Father is a **man.**

Bob will be a **man**
   when he grows up.

      (men)

man
man

Some children have nice | **manners.**
                  | ways of saying
                  | and doing things.

     (manner)

manners
man-ners
manners

Here are | **many** chickens.
        | a large number of

many
man-y
many

This is a | **map** of part of North America.
       | flat picture

     (maps)

map
map

A B C D E F G H I J K L M N O P Q R S T U V W X Y Z

A B C D E F G H I J K L (M) N O P Q R S T U V W X Y Z

maple
ma-ple
maple

A maple tree   A maple leaf

The **maple** tree makes shade.

Maple syrup is made from the sap of a maple tree.

marbles
mar-bles
marbles

These boys are playing a game with **marbles.**
(marble)

March
March

March is the third month of the year.

march
march

The play soldiers like to **march.**

They keep time with the drum.
(marches   marched   marching)

marigold
mar-i-gold
marigold

This flower is a **marigold.**

Marigolds are yellow or orange in color.
(marigolds)

mark
mark

The girl made a **mark** on the blackboard.

Tom had good **marks** on his report card.
(marks   marked   marking)

We go to the **market** to buy food.

Father buys cattle at the **market**.

A **market** is a place
where things are bought and sold.

(markets)

market
mar-ket
market

Father and Mother | were **married** long ago.
became husband and wife

When I grow up, I will **marry** someone.

(marries   married   marrying)

marry
mar-ry
marry

The children are putting on **masks**
for the Halloween party.

(mask)

masks
masks

The dog likes his | **master.**
the man who owns him.

(masters)

master
mas-ter
master

The knife and fork
are on a table **mat.**

This is a door **mat.**
We wipe our shoes on a door **mat.**

(mats)

mat
mat

A B C D E F G H I J K L M N O P Q R S T U V W X Y Z

match
match

One match   A box of matches

We use **matches** to start a fire.

(matches)

material
ma-te-ri-al
material

Paper and pencil are | drawing **materials.**
| things to draw with.

Silk and cotton cloth

are | dress **materials.**
| things dresses are made of.

Father is going to make a table.
He will get the **material** tonight.

(materials)

matted
mat-ted
matted

The baby's hair is | **matted.**
| tangled.

(mat   mats   matting)

matter
mat-ter
matter

My dog is sick.

We do not know what is | the **matter** | with him.
| wrong

may
may

Bob said, | **"May I** | have an apple?"
| **"Will you let me**

Mother said, "You **may."**

(might)

May
May

The girl's name is **May.**

The fifth month of the year is **May.**

	maybe
Maybe I can go with you. It may be that	may-be *maybe*
You have a doll. Will you give the doll to **me?**	**me** *me*
The cows are in a **meadow.** field of grass. (meadows)	**meadow** mead-ow *meadow*
We eat three times a day. The first **meal** is breakfast. The second **meal** is lunch. What is the third **meal?** (meals)	**meal** *meal*
I do not know what you **mean.** have in your mind. are thinking about. are trying to say. The boy is **mean.** not kind and pleasant. (means meant meaning)	**mean** *mean*
How long is this rope? The boys will **measure** it. see how long it is. (measures measured measuring)	**measure** meas-ure *measure*

A
B
C
D
E
F
G
H
I
J
K
L
Ⓜ
N
O
P
Q
R
S
T
U
V
W
X
Y
Z

meat
meat

This is **meat.**

We eat **meat.**

Dogs like **meat,** too.

medicine
med-i-cine
medicine

When the baby is sick,
    the doctor gives her **medicine.**

Medicine will make her well.
        (medicines)

meet
meet

When Tom heard his father coming,
        he went to **meet** him.
            (meets   met   meeting)

melon
mel-on
melon

A watermelon   A muskmelon or cantaloupe
These **melons** are good to eat.
            (melons)

melts
melts

When the sun shines on the ice,

it | **melts** it.
   | turns it back to water.

    (melts   melted   melting)

men
men

These **men** can walk fast.
            (man)

meow
me-ow
meow

The dog said, "Bow, wow."

The cat said, **"Meow, meow."**

The man is a **merchant.** / storekeeper.

(merchants)

merchant
mer-chant
merchant

The children were **merry.** / joyful.

I wish you a **merry** Christmas.
(merrier   merriest   merrily)

merry
mer-ry
merry

Bob **met** his father at the gate
to help carry the packages.
(meet   meets   meeting)

met
met

The dog says, "Bow, wow."
The kitten says, **"Mew, mew."**

mew
mew

These **mice** eat cheese.
Some **mice** are gray.
(mouse)

mice
mice

The man is talking into the **microphone.**
You can hear him
if you listen to the radio.
(microphones)

microphone
mi-cro-phone
microphone

The big bear   The middle-sized   The baby bear
bear

The girl stood in the **middle of** / half way across the road.

middle
mid-dle
middle

A B C D E F G H I J K L Ⓜ N O P Q R S T U V W X Y Z

might *might*	Mother said that I **might** go. It **might** rain tomorrow. (may)
mile *mile*	Grandfather lives in the country many **miles** away. A **mile** is a long way to go. We drive our car 30 **miles** an hour. (miles)
milk *milk*	The **milk** is in the bottle. Tom likes to drink **milk**. Cows give **milk**.
milking milk-ing *milking*	A farmer boy is **milking** the cow. (milk milks milked)
milkman milk-man *milkman*	The **milkman** brings the milk to our house. (milkmen)
milk wagon milk wag-on *milk wagon*	This is a **milk wagon**. The milkman carries milk in this wagon. (milk wagons)
milkweed milk-weed *milkweed*	This plant is a **milkweed**. There is a kind of milk in the stems. The feathery seeds fly and plant themselves. (milkweeds)

This is a Dutch wind**mill**.   This is a wind**mill**
                                          to pump water.

The farmer takes wheat to the **mill**
    to be ground into flour.
            (mills)

mill
mill

The man at the mill who grinds wheat
    for the farmer is a **miller.**
          (millers)

miller
mill-er
miller

Some people have a **million** dollars.

A **million** is a very big number.

This is the way to write one **million.** 1,000,000.
          (millions)

million
mil-lion
million

Mary | **minds** her mother.
     | does what her mother asks her to do.

Do you | **mind** | if we go?
     | care |

I do not know what you | have in **mind.**
                           | are thinking about.

    (minds   minded   minding)

mind
mind

This pencil is not yours.

It | is **mine.**
   | belongs to me.

    (my)

mine
mine

177

minute min-ute *minute*	What time is it? It is ten **minutes** past 9. There are 60 **minutes** in an hour. Wait a **minute** for me. (minutes)
miss *miss*	Mother went away. I **miss** her so much. (misses missed missing)
Miss *Miss*	This is "Little **Miss** Muffet." My sister is not married. She is **Miss** Smith. (Misses)
mistake mis-take *mistake*	I got a good mark on my paper. I made a **mistake** / gave a wrong answer on only one question. (mistakes mistook mistaking mistaken)
mistress mis-tress *mistress*	The cat likes her **mistress.** / the woman who owns her. (mistresses)
mitten mit-ten *mitten*	A **mitten** does not have a place for each finger. It has a place for the thumb. (mittens)

A
B
C
D
E
F
G
H
I
J
K
L
(M)
N
O
P
Q
R
S
T
U
V
W
X
Y
Z

See Mother | mix | the cake.
         | stir |

(mixes   mixed   mixing)

mix
mix

Father will be here in a | **moment.** |
                         | very short time. |

(moments)

moment
mo-ment
moment

Monday is the second day of the week.

Monday
Mon-day
Monday

This is **money.**

We buy things with **money.**

money
mon-ey
money

This is a **monkey.**
Monkeys have long tails.
(monkeys)

monkey
mon-key
monkey

When is your birthday?
Mine is in the **month** of May.
There are 12 **months** in a year.
May is the fifth **month.**
(months)

month
month

The lamb says, "Ba, ba, ba."

The cow says, **"Moo, moo, moo."**

moo
moo

The **moon** shines brightly at night.
(moons)

moon
moon

A B C D E F G H I J K L Ⓜ N O P Q R S T U V W X Y Z

179

moonlight
moon-light
moonlight

The children sat in the **moonlight.**
light made by the moon.

---

more
more

Jack liked the candy I gave him.

He said, "Please give me some **more.**"

(most)

---

morning
morn-ing
morning

I go to bed at night.

I get up in the **morning.**

(mornings)

---

morning glory
morn-ing glo-ry
morning glory

This flower is a **morning glory.**

It blossoms early in the morning.

Then it closes up for the rest
of the day.

(morning-glories)

---

moss
moss

Moss is a green plant.

It grows close to the ground
and sometimes on trees.

It is soft like velvet.

---

most
most

Jane has some apples.

Mary has more apples
than Jane has.

Jack has the **most** of all.

(more)

This is a **moth.**

It looks like a butterfly.

Moths fly at night.

(moths)

moth
moth

I live at home with my **mother** and father.

Mother takes care of me.

(mothers)

mother
moth-er
mother

Some people cannot hear.

They talk by making **motions** with their fingers.

Tom will come here if I **motion** to him.

(motions   motioned   motioning)

motion
mo-tion
motion

This is a **mountain.**

A **mountain** is a big hill.

(mountains)

mountain
moun-tain
mountain

This is a **mouse.**

A **mouse** is not as big as a rat.

(mice)

mouse
mouse

Baby put a spoon in her **mouth.**

She likes to feed herself.

(mouths)

mouth
mouth

A B C D E F G H I J K L Ⓜ N O P Q R S T U V W X Y Z

move
move

The baby is trying
to **move** the chair.

We lived in the country before we **moved**
to the city.

(moves   moved   moving)

mow
mow

Bob will **mow** the lawn.

The grass will be cut.

(mows)   (mowed)   (mowing)

Mr.
Mr.

My father is **Mr.** Brown.

Mrs.
Mrs.

My mother is **Mrs.** Brown.

much
much

Bob is sick.

He ate too **much** candy.

mud
mud

The children like to play in the **mud.**
wet earth.

They make **mud** pies.

(muddy)

This is written **music**. We sing in **music** class. I listen to **music** over the radio. **Music** is beautiful sounds.	**music** mu-sic *music*
Children **must** go to school. have to	**must** *must*
The dog has a **muzzle** over his mouth. (muzzles)	**muzzle** muz-zle *muzzle*
This is **my** book. It is mine. (mine)	**my** *my*
I read all the stories **myself**.	**myself** my-self *myself*

A
B
C
D
E
F
G
H
I
J
K
L
Ⓜ
N
O
P
Q
R
S
T
U
V
W
X
Y
Z

nail
nail

Father made a box.

He pounded the **nails** with a hammer.

A nail

Our finger**nails** help us pick up things.

(nails   nailed   nailing)

name
name

My **name** is Jack.

What is your **name?**

What is the **name** of the flower?

We **named** our baby Jane.

(names   named   naming)

nap
nap

Baby was sleepy.

She took a **nap.**
short sleep.

(naps)

napkin
nap-kin
napkin

Jane folded her **napkin**
after eating her dinner.

She put the napkin by her plate.

(napkins)

narrow
nar-row
narrow

The road is too **narrow**
not wide enough
for our car.

(narrower   narrowest)

nasturtium
nas-tur-tium
nasturtium

This flower is a **nasturtium.**

Nasturtiums are yellow and red.

(nasturtiums)

Grandfather is a **native** of America. He was born in America. (natives)	**native** na-tive *native*
Mary ate all the jam. She was a **naughty** girl. bad (naughtier naughtiest)	**naughty** naugh-ty *naughty*
The swing is **near** the house. close to (nearer nearest)	**near** *near*
The cupboard is **neat.** clean and in order. (neater neatest)	**neat** *neat*
The dog has a collar around his **neck.** Mary wears beads around her **neck.** (necks)	**neck** *neck*

A B C D E F G H I J K L M (N) O P Q R S T U V W X Y Z

need
need

John wanted to write, but he had no pencil.

He said, "I need a pencil."
must have

(needs   needed   needing)

---

needle
nee-dle
needle

Mother can sew.

This is her **needle** and thread.

(needles)

---

neighbor
neigh-bor
neighbor

Mary is a **neighbor** to Betty.
lives next door

(neighbors)

---

nest
nest

This is a bird's **nest.**

It has eggs in it.

(nests)

---

net
net

The men put a **net** over the lion.

The **net** is made of heavy rope.

Mary wears a hair **net.**

(nets)

---

never
nev-er
never

The dog ran away.

He **never** came back again.

Mother is **never** cross with me.
at no time

---

new
new

That shoe is old.

This one is **new.**

(newer   newest   newly)

Father told us the **news.** things that had happened.	**news** *news*
We read the news in the **newspaper.** Do you like the funnies in the **newspapers?** (newspapers)	**newspaper** news-pa-per *newspaper*
The boy **next** to me is Dan. nearest The teacher said, "Dan, you may read **next.**"	**next** *next*
The mouse **nibbled** the cheese. ate little bits of (nibble nibbles nibbling)	**nibbled** nib-bled *nibbled*
Mother is a **nice** woman. very pleasant Bob drew a **nice** picture. pleasing (nicer nicest nicely)	**nice** *nice*
Mother gave me a **nickel** to buy candy. A **nickel** is five cents. (nickels)	**nickel** nick-el *nickel*
It is light in the daytime. It is dark at **night.** We go to bed at **night.** (nights)	**night** *night*
I wear a **nightdress** when I go to bed. (nightdresses)	**nightdress** night-dress *nightdress*

A B C D E F G H I J K L M (N) O P Q R S T U V W X Y Z

nightgown
night-gown
nightgown

Mother put the nightgown on the baby.
nightdress

(nightgowns)

nine
nine

How many stars are here?

There are nine stars.
9

(ninth   ninety)

9

no
no

The teacher said, "No, I do not have a book for you."
I said, "I have no book to read."

nobody
no-bod-y
nobody

I thought I heard someone in the hall.
I looked out but I saw nobody.
no one.

nod
nod

When Baby is sleepy, her head begins to nod.
bow.

(nods   nodding   nodded)

noise
noise

The ball hit the window.

I heard the noise.
sound.

(noises)

none
none

Mary said, "Give me an apple, Bob."

Bob said, "I have none."
not one."

At 12 o'clock in the daytime it is **noon.**
We eat lunch at **noon.**

noon
noon

Jane cannot swim; **nor** can Mary.

I have no pencil **nor** paper.
and no

nor
nor

North

West | W | E | East

South
"Which direction are you going?" said Tom.
"I am going **north,**" said Bob.
Eskimos live in the **North.**
(northern)

north
north

I breathe through my **nose.**
(noses)

nose
nose

Mary can play with the ball.
Baby can**not** play with the ball.
Not once did she catch it.

not
not

Bob wrote Mother a **note.**
short letter.

(notes)

note
note

Jack ate all of his lunch.

He had **nothing** left on his plate.
not anything

nothing
noth-ing
nothing

A
B
C
D
E
F
G
H
I
J
K
L
M
(N)
O
P
Q
R
S
T
U
V
W
X
Y
Z

notice
no-tice
notice

I did not | **notice** | the fire engine when it passed.
see

The teacher put a **notice**
on the board.

It said, "No school tomorrow."
(notices   noticed   noticing)

November
No-vem-ber
November

The eleventh month of the year
is **November.**

Thanksgiving comes in **November.**

now
now

I can go home | **now.**
at this time.

number
num-ber
number

4 9 1 7 8 2 4 5 0

These are **numbers.**

Do you know the name of each **number?**
(numbers)

nurse
nurse

The **nurse** takes care
of sick people.
(nurses   nursed   nursing)

nut
nut

These **nuts** are good to eat.

Did you ever see a squirrel eat a **nut?**
(nuts)

This tree is an **oak.**

oak
oak

This is the leaf of an **oak** tree.
This is the seed of an **oak** tree.
It is called an acorn.
(oaks)

I eat **oat**meal for breakfast.
It is made from **oats.**
Oats are a kind of grain.
(oats)

oat
oat

Oatmeal is a breakfast food.
It is made of oats.
Oatmeal is good to eat.

oatmeal
oat-meal
oatmeal

Bob **obeys** his mother.
does what his mother tells him.
(obey   obeyed   obeying)

obeys
o-beys
obeys

An **object** is anything that you can see or touch.
A table is an **object.**
A box is an **object.**
(objects)

object
ob-ject
object

The **ocean** is a very big sea.
The water in the **ocean** is salty.
The Pilgrims crossed the **ocean** in a boat.
(oceans)

ocean
o-cean
ocean

A B C D E F G H I J K L M N O P Q R S T U V W X Y Z

o'clock
o'-clock
o'clock

What time is it?

It is 10 **o'clock.**

I go to school at 9 **o'clock.**

October
Oc-to-ber
October

OCTOBER

October is the tenth month of the year.

Halloween comes in **October.**

---

odd
odd

There are 4 boys in row 1.

There are 5 boys in row 2.

If each boy in row 1 chooses a partner

there will be one | **odd** boy | in row 2.
| boy left over |

The clown made | **an odd** | face.
| a queer-looking |

(odder   oddest)

---

of
of

Give me a box **of** candy.

My dress is made **of** silk.

---

off
off

My hat blew **off.**

The ball fell **off** the table.

---

office
of-fice
office

Business office

Doctor's office

Post office

(offices)

We play games **often.** / many times.	**often** / of-ten / *often*
Father puts **oil** into his auto. / **Oil** makes the car run well. / Castor **oil** is used for medicine. / (oils oiled oiling)	**oil** / *oil*
Grandmother is **old.** / not young. / My shoes are **old.** / not new. / (older oldest)	**old** / *old*
Mary put the dishes **on** the table.	**on** / *on*
Once upon a time there were three bears. / I will call you just **once.** / one time. / All the children ate ice cream at **once.** / the same time.	**once** / *once*
Here is **one** apple. / 1 / (ones) / **1**	**one** / *one*
This is an **onion.** / **Onions** are good to eat. / Sometimes **onions** make tears / come to the eyes. / (onions)	**onion** / on-ion / *onion*

A
B
C
D
E
F
G
H
I
J
K
L
M
N
O
P
Q
R
S
T
U
V
W
X
Y
Z

only
on-ly
only

I saw | **only** one apple.
     | just

Grandfather has two cars.

We have | **only** one.
     | one and **no more.**

---

open
o-pen
open

The door is | **open.**
     | not closed.

Bob **opened** it.
(opens   opened   opening)

---

opposite
op-po-site
opposite

Black is the **opposite** of white.

Large is the **opposite** of small.

Bob lives across the street from me.

His house is **opposite** mine.

(opposites)

---

or
or

Did you choose the red dress **or** the green one?

Do you like apples **or** oranges best?

You must go now **or** you will be late.

---

orange
or-ange
orange

This is an **orange.**

I like **oranges** better
than any other fruit.

(oranges)

The spaceship made one **orbit** around the earth.

| circular path |

An astronaut **orbited** the earth in his spaceship.

(orbits   orbiting)

orbit
or-bit
orbit

Apples, pears, and peaches grow in our **orchard.**

Fruits grow in **orchards.**

(orchards)

orchard
or-chard
orchard

---

1   2   3   4   5

These numbers are in **order.**

They follow each other as they should.

Mother put the house in **order.**

She placed things where they belonged.

(orders   ordered   ordering)

order
or-der
order

Tom's sister played the **organ** at the church.

(organs)

organ
or-gan
organ

Rain, rain, go away.

Come again some **other** day.
| a different |

other
oth-er
other

You **ought** to go to school.
| should |

ought
ought

A B C D E F G H I J K L M N **O** P Q R S T U V W X Y Z

our
our

Father brought us a cat.

It is **our cat** now.
belongs to us

(ours)

ourselves
our-selves
ourselves

This is our kite.

We made it all by **ourselves.**

out
out

A gentleman came to see Father.

Father was out.
away.
not in.

The bird flew in the window and **out** again.

outdoors
out-doors
outdoors

We do not play ball in the house.

We play ball **outdoors.**

outside
out-side
outside

One apple is inside the basket.

Two apples are **outside** the basket.

oven
ov-en
oven

Mother put the cake
in the **oven** to bake.

(ovens)

The airplane flew **over** the house.

The show | is **over.**
| has ended.

over
o-ver
over

Mary did not pay for the milk.

She | **owes** | the grocer some money.
| has to pay |

Do you **owe** the grocer any money?

(owes   owed   owing)

owe
owe

This bird is an **owl.**

It says, "Whoo, whoo."

Owls look for their food at night.
(owls)

owl
owl

Jack gave me this ball.

It is my **own** now.

Bob | **owns** | a bicycle.
| has |

(owns   owned   owning)

own
own

An **ox** looks like a cow.

The farmer drives the **ox.**

It helps him with his work.

(oxen)

ox
ox

A
B
C
D
E
F
G
H
I
J
K
L
M
N
Ⓞ
P
Q
R
S
T
U
V
W
X
Y
Z

A B C D E F G H I J K L M N O P Q R S T U V W X Y Z

pa *pa*	**Pa** is another name for Father.
pack *pack*	We are going away. Mother will **pack** our clothes in the bag. put together (packs packed packing)
packages pack-ages *packages*	See the **packages** under the Christmas tree. things wrapped up (package)
pad *pad*	This is a **pad** of paper. tablet This is a **pad** for the baby's carriage. (pads)
page *page*	The book is opened to **page** 11. Read the story on **page** 11. (pages)
pail *pail*	This is a **pail.** bucket. (pails)

Baby burned her hand. It **pained** her very much. hurt Did you ever have a **pain** from being burned? (pains pained paining)	**pain** *pain*
See the man **painting** the house. He is using white **paint.** (paints painted painting)	**paint** *paint*
This is one shoe. This is a **pair** of shoes. He bought a **pair** of shoes for me. (pairs)	**pair** *pair*
This is a pair of **pajamas.** Some people sleep in nightdresses. Others wear **pajamas.**	**pajamas** pa-ja-mas *pajamas*
This house is a **palace.** A king lives in a **palace.** (palaces)	**palace** pal-ace *palace*
When Mother cut her finger, her face became **pale.** whitish. (paler palest)	**pale** *pale*
This is a **palm** tree. The **palm** of the hand is the inside of the hand. (palms)	**palm** *palm*

A B C D E F G H I J K L M N O (P) Q R S T U V W X Y Z

pan
pan

This is a **pan.**
Mother cooks pudding in a **pan.**
(pans)

pancake
pan-cake
pancake

Mother fried these **pancakes** for my breakfast.
Did you ever eat a **pancake**
with butter and syrup on it?
(pancakes)

pansy
pan-sy
pansy

This flower is a **pansy.**
Pansies are of many colors.
Some **pansies** look like faces.
(pansies)

pant
pant

The dog is warm and tired.
See him **pant.**
breathe fast and hard.
(pants   panted   panting)

pants
pants

This is a pair of boy's **pants.**
trousers.

papa
pa-pa
papa

That man is Bob's **papa.**
father.
(papas)

paper
pa-per
paper

We write on **paper.**
Books are made of **paper.**
We wrap things in **paper.**
We read the news**papers.**
(papers)

This man jumped from an airplane in the **parachute**. (parachutes)	**parachute** par-a-chute *parachute*
The circus **parade** is marching by. (parades paraded parading)	**parade** pa-rade *parade*
When Mary ran into Bob she said, "I beg your **pardon.**" "Excuse me."	**pardon** par-don *pardon*
Everyone has two **parents**. Your father is one **parent**. Your mother is the other **parent**. (parents)	**parent** par-ent *parent*
See Father **park** the car. The children play in the **park**. (parks parked parking)	**park** *park*
Bob had a whole apple. He gave Mary a **part** / piece of it. Mary took **part** in the show. (parts)	**part** *part*

A B C D E F G H I J K L M N O **P** Q R S T U V W X Y Z

A
B
C
D
E
F
G
H
I
J
K
L
M
N
O
(P)
Q
R
S
T
U
V
W
X
Y
Z

party
par-ty
party

Jane had a birthday **party.**

She asked seven boys and girls to her **party.**

(parties)

pass
pass

The big car will | **pass** | the small one.
| go by |

See Jack | **pass** | the books.
| hand out |

(passes   passed   passing)

past
past

Mother went | **past** | the window.
| by |

paste
paste

A jar of paste

We use **paste** to stick things together.

(pastes   pasted   pasting)

pasture
pas-ture
pasture

Cows eat grass in the | **pasture.**
| grassy field.

(pastures)

See me **pat** the horse
tap
with my hand.
(pats   patted   patting)

pat
pat

Father tore a hole in his coat.

Mother sewed a **patch**
piece of cloth
over the hole.
(patches   patched   patching)

patch
patch

There is a **path**
narrow road
through the woods.
(paths)

path
path

Hear the **patter, patter** of the rain
tap, tap
on the windowpane.
(patters   pattered   pattering)

patter
pat-ter
patter

Grandmother will make a new dress for me.

She will buy a paper **pattern** today.

She will cut the dress just like the paper **pattern.**
(patterns)

pattern
pat-tern
pattern

The dog held up his **paw.**
foot.
(paws)

paw
paw

A
B
C
D
E
F
G
H
I
J
K
L
M
N
O
Ⓟ
Q
R
S
T
U
V
W
X
Y
Z

A
B
C
D
E
F
G
H
I
J
K
L
M
N
O
Ⓟ
Q
R
S
T
U
V
W
X
Y
Z

pay
pay

Tom bought some candy.

He had to **pay** a nickel for it.
give

(pays   paid   paying)

peas
peas

There are seven **peas** in this pod.

Peas are good to eat.

(pea)

peach
peach

A peach

A **peach** is a fruit.

Peaches are good to eat.

(peaches)

peacock
pea-cock
peacock

This bird is a **peacock.**

He has beautiful feathers.

(peacocks)

peanuts
pea-nuts
peanuts

I like to eat **peanuts.**

Squirrels like **peanuts,** too.

Peanuts grow in the ground.

(peanut)

pear
pear

A **pear** is a fruit.

Pears are sweet and juicy.

(pears)

Father bought a **peck** of potatoes.
eight quarts

A woodpecker **pecks**
taps with his bill

on the trees.
(pecks   pecked   pecking)

peck
peck

The little chicken says, **"Peep, peep."**

Mother **peeped** through the door
looked

to see if the baby was asleep.
(peeps   peeped   peeping)

peep
peep

This is a **pen**   This is a **pen**
to keep the pig in.   to write with.
(pens)

pen
pen

Sometimes we write with a pen
and sometimes with a **pencil.**
(pencils)

pencil
pen-cil
pencil

I can buy candy with this **penny.**

A **penny** is one cent.
(pennies)

penny
pen-ny
penny

A
B
C
D
E
F
G
H
I
J
K
L
M
N
O
(P)
Q
R
S
T
U
V
W
X
Y
Z

ABCDEFGHIJKLMNOP QRSTUVWXYZ

people
peo-ple
people

See these **people.**
men and women, boys and girls.

perfect
per-fect
perfect

Mary's paper was **perfect.**
had no mistakes.

(perfectly)

perhaps
per-haps
perhaps

If you are good **perhaps** you may go.
maybe

period
pe-ri-od
period

A **period** is the dot used at the end of a sentence.

(periods)

person
per-son
person

There isn't a **person** in the room.
man, woman, or child

(persons)

pet
pet

These animals are my **pets.**

I love my **pets** and take care of them.

Do you have a **pet?**

(pets   petted   petting)

petal
pet-al
petal

This is a rose.   This is a **petal** from the rose.

(petals)

This flower is a **petunia**. **Petunias** are bright-colored. (petunias)	**petunia** pe-tu-ni-a *petunia*
This is a **piano**. I can play the **piano**. Its music is sweet. (pianos)	**piano** pi-an-o *piano*
See Bob **pick** apples. gather (picks picked picking)	**pick** *pick*
This is a jar of **pickles**. Some **pickles** are sweet and some are sour. (pickle)	**pickles** pick-les *pickles*
These children are having a **picnic**. It is an outdoor party. We eat outdoors at a **picnic**. (picnics picnicked picnicking)	**picnic** pic-nic *picnic*
This is a **picture** of trees. Did you ever have your **picture** taken? (pictures)	**picture** pic-ture *picture*

A B C D E F G H I J K L M N O (P) Q R S T U V W X Y Z

pie
pie

This is a **pie.**
What kind of **pie** do you like best?

(pies)

piece
piece

This is a whole pie. This is a **piece** of a pie.
part

(pieces)

pierced
pierced

Bob **pierced** a hole in the paper.
punched

(pierce   pierces   piercing)

pig
pig

This is a **pig.**
The meat of a **pig** is called
pork or ham.

(pigs)

pigeon
pi-geon
pigeon

This bird is a **pigeon.**
dove.

Some people have pet **pigeons.**

(pigeons)

This is a **pile** of sand.

This is a **pile** of wood.
Father **piled** the wood.
He put it in order.
(piles   piled   piling)

pile
pile

The doctor gave Tom some | **pills.**
| balls of medicine.

A **pill** is easy to take.
(pills)

pill
pill

The baby's head is on the **pillow.**
(pillows)

pillow
pil-low
pillow

This man drives an airplane.
He is a **pilot.**
(pilots)

pilot
pilot

These **pins** are used to fasten things together.
(pin   pinned   pinning)

pins
pins

We use **pine** trees for Christmas trees.
Their leaves are called needles.
Their seeds grow in cones.
The needles stay on all winter.
(pines)

pine
pine

A
B
C
D
E
F
G
H
I
J
K
L
M
N
O
Ⓟ
Q
R
S
T
U
V
W
X
Y
Z

pineapple
pine-ap-ple
pineapple

This is a **pineapple.**
Pineapple is a fruit.
It is good to eat.
(pineapples)

pink
pink

The baby has **pink** cheeks.
light red

pint
pint

The larger bottle is a quart.
The smaller bottle is a **pint.**
A **pint** is one half as much
as a quart.
(pints)

pipe
pipe

This is a **pipe**
for Father to smoke.
(pipes)

This is a water **pipe.**

pits
pits

The hard stones in cherries,
peaches, and other fruits are
called **pits** or stones.
(pit)

pitcher
pitch-er
pitcher

This is a water **pitcher.**

The boy pitches the ball.
He is the **pitcher.**
(pitchers)
(pitch   pitches   pitched   pitching)

The book is in its **place.**
where it belongs.

Bob **placed** the book on the table.
put

(places   placed   placing)

place
place

Bob understood the directions for making the box.

The directions were **plain.**
clear.

Mary has on a **plain** dress.

It has no trimmings.
(plainer   plainest   plainly)

plain
plain

The boys will **plan** their work
think out a way to do

before they start to work.

The boys have a **plan** that tells
drawing

how to make a kite.
(plans   planned   planning)

plan
plan

This is a **plane.**
Father uses it
to make the wood smooth.

This is an air**plane.**
(planes   planed   planing)

plane
plane

A
B
C
D
E
F
G
H
I
J
K
L
M
N
O
(P)
Q
R
S
T
U
V
W
X
Y
Z

plant
plant

This is a **plant** in a pot.

The farmer | **plants** the corn.
puts the corn in the ground.

(plants   planted   planting)

plaster
plas-ter
plaster

The walls are covered with **plaster**.

Wallpaper is put on over the **plaster**.

(plasters   plastered   plastering)

plate
plate

This is a **plate**.

A **plate** is a flat dish.

I eat from a **plate**.

(plates)

platform
plat-form
platform

This is a **platform**.

It is like a little stage.

It is higher than the floor.

(platforms)

play
play

Father likes to work.

I do not like to work

but I like to | **play.**
have fun.

(plays   played   playing)
(player   playful)

Bob plays baseball.

He is a baseball **player.**

(players)

player
play-er
player

The children play in the **playhouse.**
small house.

(playhouses)

playhouse
play-house
playhouse

Mary has two **playmates.**
children to play with.

Do you have a playmate?

(playmates)

playmate
play-mate
playmate

We had a **pleasant** time on our picnic.
happy

pleasant
pleas-ant
pleasant

Mary is polite.

She said, **"Please** give me an apple."

Bob tries to **please** his mother.
make his mother glad.

(pleases   pleased   pleasing)

please
please

It is a **pleasure** to see you.
joy

(pleasures)

pleasure
pleas-ure
pleasure

A
B
C
D
E
F
G
H
I
J
K
L
M
N
O
(P)
Q
R
S
T
U
V
W
X
Y
Z

plenty
plen-ty
plenty

We have **plenty** of books for the class.
all the books we need

plow
plow

The farmer uses this **plow**

for **plowing.**
turning over the ground.

(plows   plowed   plowing)

plum
plum

This is a **plum.**

A **plum** is a fruit.

Plums are red, green, yellow, or purple.

They are good to eat.
(plums)

plump
plump

The baby is **plump.**
fat.

pocket
pock-et
pocket

The boy put his hand in his **pocket.**
(pockets)

pod
pod

These are peas in a **pod.**

The cover is called a **pod.**
(pods)

This is a **poem**.

Little boy, little boy,
Down by the tree,
I like the bird house
You made for me.
(poems)

poem
po-em
poem

My pencil has a **point**.
sharp end

Mother told me
to **point** to the tree.
put my finger toward

(points   pointed   pointing)

point
point

This sign means **poison**.
Some drugs are **poison**.
Do not touch things
with the **poison** sign on them.
They may hurt you.
(poisons   poisoned   poisoning)

poison
poi-son
poison

This is a **polar** bear.
He is white.
He came from a very cold land.
(polar bears)

polar bear
po-lar bear
polar bear

The flag is fastened
to the **flagpole**.
(poles)

pole
pole

A
B
C
D
E
F
G
H
I
J
K
L
M
N
O
(P)
Q
R
S
T
U
V
W
X
Y
Z

policeman
po-lice-man
policeman

This is a **policeman.**

He is a helper.

He sees that people obey the rules
of the country.

(policemen)

---

polite
po-lite
polite

Tom is **polite.**
has good manners.

(politeness   politely)

---

pond
pond

Father went fishing in the **pond.**

A **pond** is a small lake.

(ponds)

---

pony
po-ny
pony

See Tom's **pony.**
It is not as big as a horse.

(ponies)

---

pop
pop

John broke his balloon.

We could hear it **pop.**

Popcorn **pops** when it gets hot.
bursts open

(pops   popped   popping)

---

popcorn
pop-corn
popcorn

Popcorn is corn that pops open when it gets hot.

It is good to eat.

This is a **poplar** tree.

See how tall and thin it is.

(poplars)

poplar
pop-lar
poplar

This flower is a **poppy**.

Poppies are of many colors.

(poppies)

poppy
pop-py
poppy

Baby is on the **porch**.

(porches)

porch
porch

Pork is a kind of meat.

Pork comes from pigs.

pork
pork

The three bears ate **porridge**.

Goldilocks ate up all the **porridge.**
breakfast food.

porridge
por-ridge
porridge

This man is a **porter**.

He carries people's bags for them.

(porters)

porter
por-ter
porter

I will go if **possible.**
it can be done.

possible
pos-si-ble
possible

The gate is fastened to a **post**.

I will **post** Grandma's letter.
mail

(posts   posted   posting)

post
post

A
B
C
D
E
F
G
H
I
J
K
L
M
N
O
Ⓟ
Q
R
S
T
U
V
W
X
Y
Z

A
B
C
D
E
F
G
H
I
J
K
L
M
N
O
(P)
Q
R
S
T
U
V
W
X
Y
Z

poster
post-er
poster

Bob made this **poster.**

I will put it on the wall.

(posters)

GIVE TO XMAS FUND

postman
post-man
postman

The **postman** gave me the letter.

The **postman** takes letters to people's homes.

(postmen)

post office
post of-fice
post office

I got some stamps at the **post office.**

I mailed a letter at the **post office.**

(post offices)

pot
pot

A flower pot   A teapot   A kitchen pot

These are **pots.**

(pots)

potato
po-ta-to
potato

A white potato   A sweet potato

Potatoes grow in the ground.

They are good to eat.

(potatoes)

A **pound** of butter is as heavy as a pint of milk. Father **pounded** the nails with a hammer. (pounds pounded pounding)	**pound** *pound*
See Mary **pour** the milk into the glass. (pours poured pouring)	**pour** *pour*
Mother is putting **powder** on her face. **Powder** is fine like dust. (powders powdered powdering)	**powder** pow-der *powder*
Mary will **practice** her music lesson. play her music lesson over and over. (practices practiced practicing)	**practice** prac-tice *practice*
The teacher will **praise** your work speak well of if you try hard. (praises praised praising)	**praise** *praise*
Mary is saying her **prayers**. (prayer) (pray prayed praying)	**prayers** *prayers*

A B C D E F G H I J K L M N O (P) Q R S T U V W X Y Z

prepare
pre-pare
prepare

Mary helps Mother **prepare** the dinner. / **get the dinner ready.**

(prepares   prepared   preparing)

present
pres-ent
present

I gave Father a birthday **present.** / **gift.**

I was not in school yesterday

but I am **present** today. / **here**

(presents   presented   presenting)

president
pres-i-dent
president

In the United States the **president** is the leader.

(presidents)

press
press

See Mother **press** / **iron** Father's clothes.

Bob is **pressing** / **pushing** the doorbell.

(presses   pressed   pressing)

pretend
pre-tend
pretend

Let us **pretend** / **make believe** we are fairies.

(pretends   pretended   pretending)

pretty
pret-ty
pretty

The rose is **pretty.** / **beautiful.**

(prettier   prettiest)

What **price** did you pay for your dress? How much money (prices)	**price** *price*
We learn to read from a **primer.** first book. (primers)	**primer** prim-er *primer*
The boy is a **prince.** son of a king and queen. The **prince** ran after Cinderella. (princes)	**prince** *prince*
The girl is a **princess.** daughter of a king. The wife of a prince is a **princess, too.** (princesses)	**princess** prin-cess *princess*
These are foot**prints** in the snow. I can write my name and Mary can **print** her name. My father helps **print** books like this one. (prints printed printing)	**print** *print*
Tom won a **prize** for writing the best story. A **prize** is anything you win by doing better than anyone else. (prizes prized prizing)	**prize** *prize*

A B C D E F G H I J K L M N O ⓟ Q R S T U V W X Y Z

A
B
C
D
E
F
G
H
I
J
K
L
M
N
O
(P)
Q
R
S
T
U
V
W
X
Y
Z

promise
prom-ise
promise

Father always | keeps his **promise.**
| does what he says he will do.

(promises   promised   promising)

promote
pro-mote
promote

If you have good marks,

your teacher will | **promote** you.
| put you in a higher grade.

(promotes   promoted   promoting)

prompt
prompt

Bob is always | **prompt.**
| on time.

(promptly   promptness)

pronounce
pro-nounce
pronounce

Baby cannot | **pronounce** | many words yet.
| say plainly |

(pronounces   pronounced   pronouncing)

propeller
pro-pel-ler
propeller

The **propeller** on the airplane
goes around and around.
(propellers)

proper
prop-er
proper

It is | **proper** | to say, "Excuse me,"
| right |

when you leave the dinner table.
(properly)

The dog protects the baby.
sees that nothing harms

(protection)

(protects   protected   protecting)

protects
pro-tects
protects

Baby is **proud** of her new shoes.
thinks well

(prouder   proudest   proudly)

proud
proud

I like **puddings.**

Mother made chocolate **pudding** for dinner.

(puddings)

pudding
pud-ding
pudding

This is a powder **puff.**

Mother uses it to put powder
on her face.

The wolf huffed and he **puffed**
blew

at the little pig's house.
(puffs   puffed   puffing)

puff
puff

See the boy **pull** the wagon.

The dentist **pulled** Bob's tooth.
(pulls   pulled   pulling)

pull
pull

A
B
C
D
E
F
G
H
I
J
K
L
M
N
O
Ⓟ
Q
R
S
T
U
V
W
X
Y
Z

pumpkin
pump-kin
pumpkin

I like **pumpkin** pie.

We made a jack-o-lantern out of a **pumpkin.**

(pumpkins)

punished
pun-ished
punished

The thief will be **punished** by being put in jail.

(punish   punishes   punishing)

pupil
pu-pil
pupil

In our grade there are twenty-five | **pupils.**
| children.

I am one **pupil** and Bob is another.

(pupils)

puppy
pup-py
puppy

A baby dog is called a **puppy.**

(puppies)

pure
pure

The water in this well is | **pure.**
| clear and clean.

(purer   purest)

purple
pur-ple
purple

Purple is a color.

We make **purple** by putting red and blue together.

purr
purr

Did you ever hear a cat **purr?**

It sounds like a humming sound.

(purrs   purred   purring)

I keep my pennies in a **purse.**
(purses)

purse
purse

See the man **push** the cart.

I like to pull the cart better than
to **push** it.
(pushes   pushed   pushing)

push
push

This is a **pussy.**
cat.

pussy
puss-y
pussy

This is a **pussy willow.**

The buds along the stems are
soft like a pussy's fur.
(pussy willows)

pussy willow
puss-y wil-low
pussy willow

See Bob **put** the books
on the table.
(puts   putting)

put
put

A
B
C
D
E
F
G
H
I
J
K
L
M
N
O
Ⓟ
Q
R
S
T
U
V
W
X
Y
Z

A B C D E F G H I J K L M N O P Q R S T U V W X Y Z

quack
quack

The turkey says, "Gobble, gobble."
The duck says, **"Quack, quack."**

quarrel
quar-rel
quarrel

Bob and Mary are good children.

They never | **quarrel.**
say angry words to each other.

(quarrels   quarreled   quarreling)

quart
quart

Two pints of milk
make a **quart.**
(quarts)

quarter
quar-ter
quarter

A whole pie

A | quarter | of a pie
fourth

This is a | **quarter.**
25¢ piece.

(quarters)

queen
queen

This woman is a **queen.**

She is the king's wife.
(queens)

queer
queer

What a | **queer** | house!
strange

(queerer   queerest   queerly)

Where is your book? Can you answer this **question?** (questions)	**question** ques-tion *question*
Mother said, "Be quick about your work." fast (quicker quickest quickly)	**quick** *quick*
The children were talking loudly. The teacher told them to be **quiet.** make no noise. The children became very **quiet.** still. (quieter quietest quietly)	**quiet** qui-et *quiet*
The men quit working at 6 o'clock. stop It is **quitting** time at 6 o'clock. time to stop (quits quitting)	**quit** *quit*
The boy sang quite nicely. very Jane is not **quite** as tall as Bob. almost	**quite** *quite*
Bob is not a **quitter.** Bob does not give up easily. (quitters)	**quitter** quit-ter *quitter*

A B C D E F G H I J K L M N O P Q R S T U V W X Y Z

A
B
C
D
E
F
G
H
I
J
K
L
M
N
O
P
Q
(R)
S
T
U
V
W
X
Y
Z

rabbit
rab-bit
rabbit

This is a **rabbit.**

See his long ears and short tail.

He can jump fast.

(rabbits)

race
race

The boys ran a **race.**

They **raced** to see
who would win.

(races   raced   racing)

radio
ra-di-o
radio

Bob likes to hear music
on the **radio.**

(radios)

radish
rad-ish
radish

Tom ate the **radish.**

Some **radishes** are white, some are red.

Radishes grow in the ground.

(radishes)

rag
rag

Mother washed the dishes with a dish **rag.**
cloth.

(rags)

There is a **rail** around the porch.

A train runs on **rails.**

(rails)

rail
rail

This is a **railroad.**

The train runs on the **railroad** track.

(railroads)

railroad
rail-road
railroad

Rain is water that falls in drops.

The children are walking
in the **rain.**

It is **raining** hard.

(rains   rained   raining)

(rainy)

rain
rain

Mary sees the **rainbow** in the sky.

There are seven colors in the rainbow.

When the sun shines through the light rain,
it makes a **rainbow.**

(rainbows)

rainbow
rain-bow
rainbow

A
B
C
D
E
F
G
H
I
J
K
L
M
N
O
P
Q
Ⓡ
S
T
U
V
W
X
Y
Z

A
B
C
D
E
F
G
H
I
J
K
L
M
N
O
P
Q
Ⓡ
S
T
U
V
W
X
Y
Z

raincoat rain-coat *raincoat*	Mary is wearing a **raincoat.** It will keep her dry. (raincoats)
rainstorm rain-storm *rainstorm*	When it rains hard, we have a **rainstorm.** (rainstorms)
raise *raise*	Mary can **raise** the window. lift up (raises raised raising)
raisin rai-sin *raisin*	A **raisin** is a dried grape. I like **raisins** on cookies. (raisins)
rake *rake*	The farmer **rakes** his garden with the **rake.** (rakes raked raking)
ran *ran*	The cat **ran** after the mouse. (run runs running)
rap *rap*	See Mary **rap** on the window. knock (raps rapped rapping)

Raspberries are good to eat.

They are red.

A raspberry
(raspberries)

raspberry
rasp-ber-ry
raspberry

This is a **rat.**

It is like a mouse
but much larger.

Rats are white, gray, black, and brown.
(rats)

rat
rat

I want this doll **rather** than that one.

rather
rath-er
rather

Baby **reached** for
tried to get

the bottle with her hand.

She could not **reach** the bottle.
get to touch

(reaches   reached   reaching)

reach
reach

Betty has a book.

She can **read** in it.

She likes to **read** stories.

(reads   reading)

read
read

A
B
C
D
E
F
G
H
I
J
K
L
M
N
O
P
Q
Ⓡ
S
T
U
V
W
X
Y
Z

ready
read-y
ready

Jack could not go with us.

His hands were not washed, so he was not **ready.**

---

real
real

Baby has a toy house but we live in a **real** house.

(really)

---

reason
rea-son
reason

Bob came to school late.

His teacher said, "What is your **reason** for being late?

Why are you late?"

(reasons)

---

receive
re-ceive
receive

This is Mary's birthday.

She will | **receive** get | many gifts.

(receives   received   receiving)

---

red
red

The colors of the American flag are **red,** white, and blue.

---

redbreast
red-breast
redbreast

This bird is a | **redbreast.** robin. |

(redbreasts)

Father wound the hose

on this | reel.
frame that winds.

(reels)

reel
reel

This is a **refrigerator.**

The **refrigerator** keeps
food cold.

(refrigerators)

refrigerator
re-frig-er-a-tor
refrigerator

This is a **reindeer.**

In some lands **reindeer** are used
for work instead of horses.

reindeer
rein-deer
reindeer

The children did not | **remain** | long.
stay

I ate one apple and one | **remained.**
was left.

(remains   remained   remaining)

remain
re-main
remain

Can you **remember** what my name is?

(remembers   remembered   remembering)

remember
re-mem-ber
remember

All polite boys and men

| **remove** | their hats
take off

in the house.

(removes   removed   removing)

remove
re-move
remove

A
B
C
D
E
F
G
H
I
J
K
L
M
N
O
P
Q
®
S
T
U
V
W
X
Y
Z

A
B
C
D
E
F
G
H
I
J
K
L
M
N
O
P
Q
Ⓡ
S
T
U
V
W
X
Y
Z

rent
rent

We live in my uncle's house.

We have to pay **rent** for it.
| money for using |

(rents   rented   renting)

repeat
re-peat
repeat

Our teacher will **repeat** the question.

She will say it again.

We **repeat** doing things when we do them
again and again.

(repeats   repeated   repeating)

reply
re-ply
reply

I wrote Grandmother a letter.

I got a **reply.**

(replies   replied   replying)

report
re-port
report

Mary | gave a **report** of | her visit to the farm.
| told all about |

(reports   reported   reporting)

resident
res-i-dent
resident

Jack's father is a **resident** of | our town.
| person who lives in |

(residents)

rest
rest

Mother was tired.

She sat down to **rest.**

We ate the | **rest** of the apples.
| apples that were left. |

(rests   rested   resting)

The teacher gave Tom a book.

He will **return it** | tomorrow.
take it back

I went to town but **returned** | soon.
came back

(returns   returned   returning)

return
re-turn
return

This is a **rhyme**.

Old Mother Hubbard

Went to the cupboard.

The words cat and sat **rhyme.**
sound alike.

(rhymes   rhymed   rhyming)

rhyme
rhyme

Mary has a bow of **ribbon**
in her hair.

This is a package tied with **ribbon.**

Ribbon is made of silk or velvet.

(ribbons)

ribbon
rib-bon
ribbon

Rice grows in very wet ground.

Rice is something like wheat.

Mother makes **rice** pudding.

rice
rice

The man | is **rich.**
has much money.

(riches   richer   richest)

rich
rich

A
B
C
D
E
F
G
H
I
J
K
L
M
N
O
P
Q
Ⓡ
S
T
U
V
W
X
Y
Z

rid *rid*	The Pied Piper **rid** the town of rats. took the rats from the town. (rids ridding riddance)
riddles rid-dles *riddles*	The children were playing games. They were guessing **riddles.** (riddle)
ride *ride*	Bob **rides** a horse. Tom **rides** a bicycle. I **ride** in the car with **Father.** (rides rode riding)
rider rid-er *rider*	Bob **rides** a horse. He is a good **rider.** (riders)
right *right*	Bob writes with his left hand. Mary writes with her **right** hand. This picture is wrong. This picture is **right.**

The outer covering of an orange is called the **rind.**

Lemons have **rinds,** too.

(rinds)

rind
rind

Jane's **ring** is made of gold.

See Bob **ring** the bell.
It sounds loud.

(rings   rang   rung   ringing)

ring
ring

The apple is | **ripe.**
ready to be eaten.

(riper   ripest)
(ripen   ripens   ripened   ripening)

ripe
ripe

The boys watched the sun | **rise.**
come up.

We | **rise** | when we read aloud.
stand up

(rises   rose   rising   risen)

rise
rise

The boat sails down the **river.**

The water in the **river** moves along
in one direction.

(rivers)

river
riv-er
river

A
B
C
D
E
F
G
H
I
J
K
L
M
N
O
P
Q
Ⓡ
S
T
U
V
W
X
Y
Z

road
road

We did not know the | **road**
way to take |

to get to my grandmother's.

The auto stood in the middle of the **road.**

(roads)

---

roar
roar

The dog barks but the lion | **roars.**
makes a big noise. |

Did you ever hear a lion **roar?**

(roars   roared   roaring)

---

roast
roast

Mother put the meat in the oven to | **roast.**
cook. |

(roasts   roasted   roasting)

---

robbed
robbed

The bad dog | **robbed** the cat of her supper.
stole the cat's supper. |

(rob   robs   robbing)
(robber   robbers)

---

robin
rob-in
robin

This bird is a **robin.**

The **robin's** breast is red.

(robins)

---

rock
rock

A rock or stone

See Mother **rock** the baby.

(rocks   rocked   rocking)

This is a space **rocket**.
Spaceships are **rocketed**
  into space.
   (rockets   rocketing)

rocket
rock-et
rocket

Bob has a fishing **rod.**
                   pole.
   (rods)

rod
rod

The boys **roll** the snowball.
         turn the snowball **over and over.**

A **roll** is a kind of bread.

I like sweet **rolls.**
   (rolls   rolled   rolling)

roll
roll

The fireman is on the **roof.**
                      top of the house.
   (roofs)

roof
roof

How many **rooms** do you have in your house?

We sleep in the bed**room.**

We eat in the dining **room**

There is not enough **room** for everyone to play
                     space
  at one time.
   (rooms)

room
room

This chicken is not a hen.

He is a **rooster.**
   (roosters)

rooster
roost-er
rooster

roots
roots

The **roots** of the plants are in the ground.

Roots help plants get food and water from the ground.

(root)

rope
rope

Children like to jump the **rope**.

We use a **rope** to tie up the dog.

(ropes)

rose
rose

This flower is a **rose**.

It grows on a bush.

Some **roses** climb on frames.

(roses)

rosebush
rose-bush
rosebush

The rose grows on a **rosebush.**

(rosebushes)

rough
rough

Paper is smooth.

The sidewalk is **rough.**

(rougher   roughest   roughly)

round
round

A ball is **round.**   A circle is **round.**

The man plants his garden in **rows.**

See Bob **row** the boat.
(rows   rowed   rowing)

Did you ever **rub** your hands together
    to get warm?

Father **rubbed** his face with a towel.

My hands were not clean.

I **rubbed** them hard to get them clean.
(rubs   rubbed   rubbing)

Overshoes are made of **rubber.**

Tires are made of **rubber.**

Erasers are made of **rubber.**

Rubber is made from sap.

The sap comes from **rubber** trees.
(rubbers)

The man | was **rude.**
       | had poor manners.
(ruder   rudest   rudely)

ruffle
ruf-fle
ruffle

This is a plain curtain.

(ruffles)

This is a curtain with a **ruffle** around it.

rug
rug

There is a **rug** on the floor.

(rugs)

ruin
ru-in
ruin

If you get paint on your suit, it will **ruin** / spoil it.

(ruins   ruined   ruining)

rule
rule

This is a **rule.** / ruler.

The children wanted to play a new game.
The teacher read the **rules** which told them how to play it.

The king **rules** / leads his country.

(rules   ruled   ruling)

ruler
rul-er
ruler

This is a **ruler.** / rule.

The king is the **ruler** / leader of a country.

(rulers)

See the children **run**.
Some children can **run** fast.
   (runs   ran   running)

run

Did you see the children **rush** out of the room?
hurry
   (rushes   rushed   rushing)

rush

Rye bread is made from rye flour.
Rye is something like wheat.

rye

A
B
C
D
E
F
G
H
I
J
K
L
M
N
O
P
Q
Ⓡ
S
T
U
V
W
X
Y
Z

A
B
C
D
E
F
G
H
I
J
K
L
M
N
O
P
Q
R
(S)
T
U
V
W
X
Y
Z

sack *sack*	This is a **sack** of potatoes. (sacks)
sad *sad*	Bob could not go to the party. This made him feel **sad.** unhappy. (sadder saddest sadly)
saddle sad-dle *saddle*	The horse has a **saddle.** seat for the rider. (saddles)
safe *safe*	Cross the street when the light is green. You are **safe** then. out of danger (safer safest safely safety) This is a **safe** to keep money in. (safes)
said *said*	Father asked me to help him. I **said,** "I will be glad to help you." (say says saying)
sail *sail*	This is a boat with a **sail** on it. The wind blows against the **sail.** The wind makes the boat go. Did you ever **sail** on a big boat? travel (sails sailed sailing)

This man is a **sailor**. He sails on big boats. (sailors)	**sailor** sail-or *sailor*
Bob shoveled the snow for Father's **sake.** to help Father.	**sake** *sake*
I like pineapple **salad**. Father likes lettuce **salad**. **Salad** has **salad** dressing on it. **Salads** are made with fruit, meats, and vegetables. (salads)	**salad** sal-ad *salad*
Grandma's house is for **sale.** to be sold. Mother bought my dress at a **sale**. She did not pay much for it. (sales)	**sale** *sale*
This fish is a **salmon**. We eat **salmon**. **Salmon** is put into cans and sold at the stores.	**salmon** salm-on *salmon*
There is **salt** in the salt shaker. We put **salt** on potatoes to make them taste good. (salty)	**salt** *salt*
These houses are just the **same.** alike.	**same** *same*

A B C D E F G H I J K L M N O P Q R **S** T U V W X Y Z

A B C D E F G H I J K L M N O P Q R **S** T U V W X Y Z

sand
sand

The children like to play
in the **sand** by the lake.

Sand is tiny pieces of rock.

(sandy)

---

sandman
sand-man
sandman

The **sandman** is a make-believe man.

The **sandman** comes when we are sleepy.

---

sandwich
sand-wich
sandwich

Mother put meat between the bread.

This meat made a **sandwich.**

Sometimes she makes jelly or lettuce **sandwiches.**

(sandwiches)

---

sandy
sand-y
sandy

The floor is | **sandy.**
covered with sand.

---

sang
sang

The boy **sang** a song.

Do you like to **sing?**

(sing   sings   singing   sung)

Santa Claus
San-ta Claus
Santa Claus

Santa Claus comes
on Christmas Eve.

---

sap
sap

Maple syrup is made from **sap.**

Maple **sap** is the juice of the maple tree.

Rubber is made from **sap.**

Rubber **sap** is the juice of a rubber tree.

A **sardine** is a small fish. **Sardines** are put into cans. They are good to eat. (sardines)	**sardine** sar-dine *sardine*
Mary has a **sash** around her **waist**. The **sash** is made of ribbon. (sashes)	**sash** *sash*
Bill stood up. Mary **sat** in the chair. (sit sits sitting)	**sat** *sat*
Satin is a smooth silk cloth.	**satin** sat-in *satin*
We tried hard to **satisfy** / please our teacher. (satisfies satisfied satisfying)	**satisfy** sat-is-fy *satisfy*
We do not go to school on **Saturday** or Sunday.	**Saturday** Sat-ur-day *Saturday*
Do you like applesauce? / apples cooked and sweetened? Grandmother put a sweet **sauce** over the pudding. I like tomato **sauce** on meat. (sauces)	**sauce** *sauce*

A B C D E F G H I J K L M N O P Q R (S) T U V W X Y Z

saucer
sau-cer
saucer

This is a cup and **saucer.**

The cup is in the **saucer.**

(saucers)

sauerkraut
sau-er-kraut
sauerkraut

Sauerkraut is made from cabbage.

It is good to eat.

sausage
sau-sage
sausage

We ate a **sausage** at breakfast.

(sausages)

save
save

Mary put her money in a bank.

She will $\boxed{\begin{array}{l}\textbf{save}\\ \textbf{keep}\end{array}}$ it to buy a doll.

The boy $\boxed{\begin{array}{l}\textbf{saved} \text{ the baby's life.}\\ \textbf{kept} \text{ the baby from dying.}\end{array}}$

(saves   saved   saving)

saw
saw

This **saw** cuts wood.
(saws)

Yesterday I **saw** a black cat.
(see   sees   seeing   seen)

sawdust
saw-dust
sawdust

Sawdust is little bits of wood.

When we saw a board it makes **sawdust.**

I could not hear what you said. Please **say** it again. (says said saying)	**say** *say*
Bob is standing on the **scale.** He is getting weighed. Chickens are covered with feathers. Fish are covered with **scales.** (scales)	**scale** *scale*
The kitten has scarcely / hardly enough to eat.	**scarcely** scarce-ly *scarcely*
The dog barked at Father but it did not scare / frighten him. (scares scared scaring)	**scare** *scare*

The farmer puts a **scarecrow**
    in his garden.
A **scarecrow** scares the birds away.
    (scarecrows)
	scarecrow
	scare-crow
	scarecrow

The boy has a woolen **scarf**
    around his neck.
It will keep him warm.
 	
    Mother put a long scarf / cover
 	
    on the table.
    (scarves   scarfs)
	scarf
	scarf

A B C D E F G H I J K L M N O P Q R (S) T U V W X Y Z

A B C D E F G H I J K L M N O P Q R (S) T U V W X Y Z

scatter
scat-ter
scatter

Grandfather **scattered** the grass seeds.

He threw the grass seeds here and there.
(scatters   scattered   scattering)

scene
scene

A **scene** is a part of a play.

Each **scene** tells the time, the place,
and what is happening.
(scenes)

school
school

We go to **school** to learn.

In our **school** we have twenty teachers.
(schools)

schoolhouse
school-house
schoolhouse

This is a **schoolhouse.**

We go to school
in a **schoolhouse.**
(schoolhouses)

schoolroom
school-room
schoolroom

A **schoolroom** is a room
in the schoolhouse
where children are taught.
(schoolrooms)

scissors
scis-sors
scissors

These are **scissors.**

We cut paper and cloth with scissors.

Bob was a good boy in school.

The teacher did not scold / find fault with him.

(scolds   scolded   scolding)

Mother uses this **scoop** to take flour out of the can.

Baby likes to **scoop** the sand into the pail.

(scoops   scooped   **scooping**)

See Bob ride his **scooter.**

(scooters)

When Mary ironed her doll's dress,

she tried not to scorch / burn it.

(scorches   scorched   scorching)

Our side won because we had

the biggest score. / number of points.

We scored / made a point in the last minute of the game.

(scores   scored   scoring)

The kitchen sink was dirty.

Mother had to scour it / rub it hard to get it clean.

(scours   scoured   scouring)

scold
scold

scoop
scoop

scooter
scoot-er
scooter

scorch
scorch

score
score

scour
scour

A
B
C
D
E
F
G
H
I
J
K
L
M
N
O
P
Q
R
(S)
T
U
V
W
X
Y
Z

A
B
C
D
E
F
G
H
I
J
K
L
M
N
O
P
Q
R
Ⓢ
T
U
V
W
X
Y
Z

scrap
scrap

Tom's dog was hungry.

Tom gave him a scrap of meat.
small piece

Mother saves scraps for the chickens.
bits of leftover food

(scraps   scrapped   scrapping)

scrapbook
scrap-book
scrapbook

Mary cut out pictures and stories.
She pasted them

in her **scrapbook.**
book for pictures and stories.

(scrapbooks)

scrape
scrape

Bob got paint on his book.

He tried to scrape it off with a knife.
rub

(scrapes   scraping   scraped)

scratch
scratch

The cat tried to scratch the rug
dig

with its claws.

I have a scratch on my hand.
little cut

When Mary's arm itches, she **scratches it.**

(scratches   scratched   scratching)

scream
scream

Mary was surprised.

Did you hear her scream?
loud cry?

(screams   screaming   screamed)

Father is putting the **screen**
on the window.

It will keep the flies out.

We see the moving picture on a **screen.**

There is a **screen** in front of the fireplace.
(screens   screened   screening)

screen
screen

This is a **screw.**

It is a kind of nail.

You can pound a nail into a board.

You must turn a **screw** to get it into a board.
(screws   screwed   screwing)

screw
screw

We will ┌─────┐ the floor.
        │**scrub**│
        │wash │
        └─────┘

You must ┌─────┐ your hands hard.
         │**scrub**│
         │rub │
         └─────┘

(scrubs   scrubbed   scrubbing)

scrub
scrub

The boat is on the **sea.**

The **sea** is not as large as the ocean.

The water in the **sea** is salty.
(seas)

sea
sea

A
B
C
D
E
F
G
H
I
J
K
L
M
N
O
P
Q
R
(S)
T
U
V
W
X
Y
Z

seal
seal

These are **seals.**

They live in the ocean.

(seals)

seasick
sea-sick
seasick

Some people get sick when they ride
   on a boat at sea.

The rocking of the boat makes them **seasick.**

(seasickness)

season
sea-son
season

Winter and summer are | **seasons** of the year.
| times |

Spring and autumn are seasons of the year, too.

Which **season** do you like best?

(seasons)

seat
seat

A chair   A bench   A school seat

These are **seats.**

We sit on **seats.**

(seats   seated   seating)

second
sec-ond
second

Bob is the first child in the line.

Mary is the | **second** child.
| next child after Bob.

I hear with my ears. I **see** with my eyes. (sees saw seeing seen)	**see** *see*
Plants and flowers grow from **seeds.** The farmer plants the **seeds** in the ground. Did you ever see a **seed** in an orange? <center>(seeds)</center>	**seed** *seed*
The cat did not seem sick. look (seems seemed seeming)	**seem** *seem*
Jack's dog ran away. Have you **seen** it anywhere? (see sees saw seeing)	**seen** *seen*
The children are playing on the **seesaw.** The **seesaw** goes up and down. <center>(seesaws)</center>	**seesaw** see-saw *seesaw*
See the hungry dog seize the bone. take hold of (seizes seized seizing)	**seize** *seize*

A
B
C
D
E
F
G
H
I
J
K
L
M
N
O
P
Q
R
Ⓢ
T
U
V
W
X
Y
Z

A
B
C
D
E
F
G
H
I
J
K
L
M
N
O
P
Q
R
(S)
T
U
V
W
X
Y
Z

seldom sel-dom *seldom*	**Seldom** does Father scold me. Not very often
select se-lect *select*	If you will **select** / pick out the dress you want, Mother will buy it for you. (selects selected selecting)
self *self*	Tom had two apples. He gave one to me and kept one for him**self**. (selves)
selfish self-ish *selfish*	**Selfish** children think of themselves first. Jack was **selfish**. He kept all the candy for himself.
sell *sell*	My father owns a store. He will **sell** you some oranges for a quarter. (sells sold selling)
send *send*	If Mother needs bread from the store, she will **send me** for it. ask me to go Father **sent** Mother some flowers. (sends sent sending)
sense *sense*	I can feel, see, hear, smell, and taste. These are called **senses**. Some people cannot smell. They have no **sense** of smell. (senses)

Can you read the first | **sentence** / thought | in the story?

sentence
sen-tence
sentence

Sentences are words put together
to tell or ask something.
(sentences)

Bob will **separate** your books from mine.

He will take mine away from yours.
(separates   separated   separating)

separate
sep-a-rate
separate

September is the ninth month of the year.

September is the first month of school.

Labor Day is the first Monday
in **September**.

September
Sep-tem-ber
September

A **servant** is a man or woman who is paid
for working in someone else's home.

Some **servants** take care of children.

Some **servants** cook and clean house.
(servants)

servant
serv-ant
servant

If you want some ice cream,

Mother will | **serve** / wait upon | you.

I am happy to | **serve** / help | you.
(serves   served   serving)

serve
serve

Mary | **set** / put | the cup on the table.

(sets   setting)

set
set

A
B
C
D
E
F
G
H
I
J
K
L
M
N
O
P
Q
R
Ⓢ
T
U
V
W
X
Y
Z

seven
sev-en
seven

Here are **seven** stars.
7

7

Count them.
(seventh   seventy)

several
sev-er-al
several

Bob has **several** apples.
a few

sew
sew

Mary is making a dress for her doll.

She can **sew** with a needle and thread.

Mother can **sew** on the sewing machine.
(sews   sewed   sewing)

shade
shade

Mother is pulling down the window **shade**.

The sun cannot shine through the leaves.

It is cool in the **shade**
darker place

under the trees.
(shades   shaded   shading   shady)

shadow
shad-ow
shadow

The dog's **shadow** is the shade
made by the dog.

People, trees, and other things make **shadows**, too.
(shadows)

The children shake / rock the tree to get the apples. See these men **shake** hands. (shakes shook shaking shaken)	**shake** *shake*
Tomorrow I **shall** give you some ice cream. I **shall** go to town this afternoon.	**shall** *shall*
The **shamrock** is a kind of clover. It has three leaves. (shamrocks)	**shamrock** sham-rock *shamrock*
The **shape** of a circle is round. The **shape** of a pencil is round and long. (shapes shaped shaping)	**shape** *shape*
Mary did not have any pudding. Bob gave her his share. / part. Tom **shared** his apple with Jane. He gave Jane a part of his apple. (shares shared sharing)	**share** *share*
I cut my finger with the knife. The knife was very **sharp**. Father had just **sharpened** it. (sharper sharpest) (sharpen sharpened sharpening)	**sharp** *sharp*

A B C D E F G H I J K L M N O P Q R (S) T U V W X Y Z

shave
shave

See Father shave his whiskers.
cut off

He looks nice after **shaving.**
(shaves   shaved   shaving)

she
she

Betty is not home now.

She will be back soon.

shears
shears

These are **shears.**
big scissors.

The farmer cuts the sheep's wool with **shears.**

shed
shed

Grandfather keeps his wagon

in a **shed.**
low building.

Chickens **shed** their feathers in spring.
lose

(sheds   shedding)

sheep
sheep

This **sheep** has long wool.

The farmer cuts its wool.

It is made into cloth and yarn.

sheet
sheet

Bob writes on a **sheet** of paper.
piece

Mother puts clean **sheets** and pillowcases
on my bed.

Bed **sheets** are made of white cloth.

(sheets)

Father put the vase of flowers
on the **shelf.**

The **shelf** is fastened to the wall.
(shelves)

shelf
shelf

The children found a **shell** on the seashore.

Little animals live in **shells.**

The outside of an egg is the **shell.**

I | **shelled** the peas.
took the peas out of the pods.

(shells   shelled   shelling)

shell
shell

The house | **shelters** | us from cold and rain.
protects

Umbrellas **shelter** us from the sun and rain.
(shelters   sheltered   sheltering)

shelter
shel-ter
shelter

She's | going to school.
She is

she's
she's

Tom likes to **shine** Father's shoes.

It makes them bright and clean.

When the sun **shines,** it makes light.
(shines   shined   shining   shone   shiny)

shine
shine

This | **ship** | crosses the ocean.
big boat

People travel on **ships.**
(ships)

ship
ship

A
B
C
D
E
F
G
H
I
J
K
L
M
N
O
P
Q
R
(S)
T
U
V
W
X
Y
Z

shirt
shirt

Men wear **shirts.**

This **shirt** has a collar on it.

(shirts)

---

shiver
shiv-er
shiver

Bob was very cold.

He began to | **shiver** | with the cold.
           | shake |

(shivers   shivered   shivering)

---

shock
shock

This is a **shock** of corn.

Farmers pile up wheat
    so it makes a **shock,** too.

(shocks)

---

shoe
shoe

This is a **shoe.**

Most **shoes** are made
    of leather.

(shoes)

---

shoemaker
shoe-mak-er
shoemaker

A man who makes shoes is a **shoemaker.**

(shoemakers)

---

shook
shook

Mother **shook** the rug
    to get the dust out of it.

(shake   shakes   shaking   shaken)

The man will **shoot** at the tree with his gun. (shoots shot shooting)	**shoot** *shoot*
Mother went to the store to **shop.** / buy things. A store is a **shop.** A place where things are made is a **shop,** too. (shops shopped shopping)	**shop** *shop*
See the children play in the sand on the **shore.** / land next to the sea. (shores)	**shore** *shore*
This pencil is long. This pencil is **short.** / not long. (shorter shortest)	**short** *short*
I like strawberry **shortcake.** It is made with biscuits and strawberries. (shortcakes)	**shortcake** short-cake *shortcake*
Some children play in the streets. They **should** / ought to play on the sidewalk.	**should** *should*

A B C D E F G H I J K L M N O P Q R (S) T U V W X Y Z

shoulders
shoul-ders
shoulders

Father is carrying the baby
on his **shoulders.**
(shoulder)

shout
shout

Mary was lost.

Father heard her **shout.**
call loudly.

(shouts   shouted   shouting)

shovel
shov-el
shovel

We use a **shovel** to **shovel** the snow
off the sidewalks.

This is a steam **shovel.**

It can lift heavy loads.
(shovels   shoveled   shoveling)

show
show

Mother will **show you** her new coat.
let you see

We are going to a picture **show.**
(shows   showed   showing   shown   showy)

shower
show-er
shower

We were caught in a **shower.**
light rain.

(showers)

shut
shut

See Bob **shut** the door.
close

(shuts   shutting)

The doctor came to see Mary.

She was | **sick.**
not well. |

(sicker   sickest)

sick
sick

The cat is on one **side** of the fence.
The dog is on the other **side.**

(sides)

side
side

Do not walk in the street.

Walk on | the **sidewalk.**
the walk at the side of the street. |

(sidewalks)

sidewalk
side-walk
sidewalk

The boy saw an airplane.

He | has good **sight.**
can see very well. |

Mother looked down the street.

Father | was out of **sight.**
could not be seen. |

sight
sight

The teacher told us to | **sign** the papers.
write our names on |

THIS WAY TO
THE ZOO

The **sign** on the pole says,
"This way to the zoo."

(signs   signed   signing   signal)

sign
sign

The children were | **silent** while
quiet |

Mary was reading.

(silently)

silent
si-lent
silent

silk
silk

Some thread is **silk.**

Some cloth is **silk.**

Mother's dress is made of **silk** cloth.

---

silver
sil-ver
silver

Silver is precious, like gold.

Some knives and forks are made of **silver.**

---

since
since

My kitty is lost.

I have not seen her | **since** morning.
| from morning until now.

---

sings
sings

Bob **sings** a song while Mary plays the piano.

Singing is making music with your voice.

(sing   sang   singing   sung   singer)

---

sink
sink

If you throw a stone into the water,

it will | **sink.**
| go to the bottom.

This is a kitchen **sink.**

We wash dishes in the **sink.**

(sinks   sank   sinking   sunk)

---

sir
sir

Baa, baa, black sheep,
Have you any wool?

Yes, | **sir,**
| **Mr.,** | yes, | **sir,**
| **Mr.,**

Three bags full.

sister
sis-ter
sister

The girl is my **sister.**

We have the same mother and father.

(sisters)

sit
sit

When I am tired, I **sit** on a chair.

(sits   sat   sitting)

six
six

Do you see **six** stars?

(sixth   sixty)   6

size
size

Father will get you some shoes.

Tell him | what **size** shoes you wear.
how big your shoes should be.

My kite is | the same **size**
just as big

as yours.

(sizes)

skate
skate

This is a roller **skate.**

This is an ice **skate.**

We **skate** on the sidewalk

We **skate** on the ice

with roller **skates.**

with ice **skates.**

(skates   skated   skating)

A B C D E F G H I J K L M N O P Q R (S) T U V W X Y Z

267

skin
skin

The outside of an apple is the **skin**.

The outside of your hand is the **skin**.

Father **skinned** his hand.
rubbed the **skin off**

(skins   skinned   skinning)

skip
skip

Can you **skip** the rope?
jump

Mother **skipped** one page of the story.
passed over

(skips   skipped   skipping)

skirt
skirt

This is a **skirt**.

It is a part of a dress.
(skirts)

sky
sky

The sun is in the **sky**.   The clouds are in the **sky**.

Stars are in the **sky** at night.

The sun makes pretty colors in the **sky**.
(skies)

slant
slant

This line stands straight up and down. |

This is a **slant** line. /

This house has a **slanting** roof.

Some houses have flat roofs.
(slants   slanted   slanting)

Do not **slap** the dog.
hit the dog with your hand.

(slaps   slapped   slapping)

slap
slap

The children like to slide downhill on a **sled.**

(sleds)

sled
sled

This baby is **sleeping.**

I **sleep** at night.

(sleeps   slept   sleeping   sleepy)

sleep
sleep

Sometimes it rains.

Sometimes tiny pieces of ice fall.

This ice is called **sleet.**

Sometimes rain and ice fall at the same time.

This is **sleet,** too.

(sleets   sleeted   sleeting)

sleet
sleet

The horse is drawing the **sleigh** over the snow.

The **sleigh** has runners to slide on like a sled.

(sleighs)

sleigh
sleigh

A B C D E F G H I J K L M N O P Q R (S) T U V W X Y Z

slice
slice

Mary ate two **slices** of bread.
flat pieces

Mother **sliced** it for her.
cut

Would you like a **slice**, too?
(slices   sliced   slicing)

slide
slide

See Bob **slide** down the **slide**.
The **slide** is smooth
so you can go fast on it.
(slides   slid   sliding)

slip
slip

Bob stepped on something smooth.

He **slipped** and he fell down.
His feet went out from under him

Did you ever **slip** on the ice?

Mary wrote her name on a **slip** of paper.
small piece

Mother wears a **slip** under her dress.
(slips   slipped   slipping)

slipper
slip-per
slipper

This is a **slipper.**
low shoe.

We wear **slippers** on our feet.
(slippers)

slow
slow

Jack is **slow.**
not fast.

He is always behind time.

I write **slowly.**
not fast.

(slower   slowest   slowly)

The fox was **sly.**
tricky.

sly
sly

Tom is big.

The baby is **small.**
little.

(smaller   smallest)

small
small

Bob cut his finger.

It made his finger **smart.**
pain him.

Father is a **smart** man.

He knows **many things.**

(smarter   smartest)

smart
smart

Mother could **smell** the cake burning.

We **smell** with our noses.

Flowers have a sweet **smell.**

(smells   smelled   smelling)

smell
smell

Mother is pleased about something.

She has a **smile** on her face.

She **smiles** when she is happy.

(smiles   smiled   smiling)

smile
smile

See the **smoke** come
out of the chimney.

Father **smokes** a pipe.

(smokes   smoked   smoking   smoky)

smoke
smoke

A B C D E F G H I J K L M N O P Q R S T U V W X Y Z

smooth
smooth

The paper is | **smooth.**
                not rough.

Mother ironed the dress to make it **smooth.**

(smooths   smoothed   smoothing)

(smoother   smoothest   smoothly)

---

snail
snail

A **snail** is a soft little animal.

He lives in this shell.

Snails move slowly.

(snails)

---

snake
snake

This is a **snake.**

He has no legs.

He crawls fast.

Some **snakes** make their nests on the ground.

(snakes)

---

sneeze
sneeze

Bob had a cold.

Father said, "Put a handkerchief over your mouth when you **sneeze.**"

Sometimes pepper makes us **sneeze.**

(sneezes   sneezed   sneezing)

---

snow
snow

In winter the **snow** falls on the trees.

Snow is white.

Yesterday it **snowed** hard.

(snows   snowed   snowing)

The boys are rolling

a **snowball.**
ball made of snow.

(snowballs)

snowball
snow-ball
snowball

These are **snowflakes.**
pieces of snow.

Each **snowflake** is different.

(snowflakes)

snowflake
snow-flake
snowflake

The boys made a **snow man.**
man of snow.

(snow men)

snow man
snow man

When the wind blows
and the snow comes down fast,
we have a **snowstorm.**

(snowstorms)

snowstorm
snow-storm
snowstorm

Bob's dog ran away **so** Father tied him to a tree.

What he told is **so.**
true.

Baby was **so** sleepy she couldn't stay awake.

so
so

This is a bar of **soap.**

Tom washed his hands
with **soap** and water.

(soapy)

soap
soap

A B C D E F G H I J K L M N O P Q R ⒮ T U V W X Y Z

A
B
C
D
E
F
G
H
I
J
K
L
M
N
O
P
Q
R
(S)
T
U
V
W
X
Y
Z

sobs
sobs

The baby **sobs** / cries when he is hungry.

(sob   sobbed   sobbing)

socks
socks

These are **socks.**

Socks are short.

Stockings are long.

Socks keep our feet warm.

(sock)

soft
soft

The floor is hard.

The pillow is **soft.**

(softer   softest   softly)

soil
soil

The farmer put the seeds in the **soil.** / ground.

If you play in the mud

you will **soil** your dress. / get your dress dirty.

(soils   soiled   soiling)

sold
sold

The grocer **sold** me an apple for two cents.

(sell   sells   selling)

soldier
sol-dier
soldier

This man is a **soldier.**
He is in the army.

(soldiers)

Father gave me **some** apples.
a number of

I had **some** soup for lunch.

some
some

The mother bear said,

"Somebody has been eating my soup."
"Someone

somebody
some-bod-y
somebody

The father bear said,

"Someone has been sitting in my chair."
"Some person

someone
some-one
someone

Father has **something** for my birthday.

I do not know what it is.

something
some-thing
something

I will see you **sometime.**
at some time.

(sometimes)

sometime
some-time
sometime

Grandmother lives **somewhere** on this street.
some place

somewhere
some-where
somewhere

The man is the father.

The woman is the mother.

The boy is their **son.**

(sons)

son
son

A
B
C
D
E
F
G
H
I
J
K
L
M
N
O
P
Q
R
(S)
T
U
V
W
X
Y
Z

song *song*	The boy is singing a **song**. The name of the **song** is "Mr. Turkey." (songs)
soon *soon*	Father will be home ⌈**soon.**⌋ ⌊in a short time.⌋ (sooner soonest)
sore *sore*	Mary burned her hand. It made a **sore** on her hand. **Sores** sometimes hurt badly. (sores)
sorry sor-ry *sorry*	I was **sorry** for the man who was hurt. Bob treated Tom badly. Then he ⌈was **sorry.**⌋ ⌊wished he had not done it.⌋ (sorrier sorriest)
sort *sort*	Bob helped ⌈**sort**⌋ the books. ⌊separate⌋ Mother **sorted** the clothes. She put all of baby's clothes together. She put all of Father's clothes together. (sorts sorted sorting)
sound *sound*	We hear the tinkling **sound** of a bell. Did you hear a ⌈**sound**⌋ at night? ⌊noise⌋ Mother's voice **sounds** as if she has a cold. (sounds sounded sounding)

A B C D E F G H I J K L M N O P Q R **S** T U V W X Y Z

Mother made tomato **soup.**

What kind of **soup** do you like?

soup
soup

Sugar is sweet.

Lemons are **sour.**

(sourer   sourest)

sour
sour

In winter birds go **south** where it is warm.

Tom lives **south** of our school.

(southern)

south
south

The farmer **sows** his grain.
plants

(sow   sowed   sowing)

sows
sows

See the books on the shelf.

There is no **space** between them.
room

Astronauts fly in **space.**
the region beyond the earth.

(spaces   spaced   spacing)

space
space

This is a **spaceship.**

Astronauts ride in **spaceships.**

(spaceships)

spaceship
space-ship
spaceship

A
B
C
D
E
F
G
H
I
J
K
L
M
N
O
P
Q
R
Ⓢ
T
U
V
W
X
Y
Z

A
B
C
D
E
F
G
H
I
J
K
L
M
N
O
P
Q
R
(S)
T
U
V
W
X
Y
Z

sparrow
spar-row
sparrow

This bird is a **sparrow.**

The **sparrow** is brown and gray.

(sparrows)

---

speak
speak

Father | **speaks** | in a deep voice.
        | talks |

I will **speak** to Mother about the party.
(speaks   spoke   speaking   spoken)

---

speck
speck

Mary got a | **speck** | of dirt on her dress.
            | little spot |

(specks)

---

speckled
speck-led
speckled

This is a **speckled** egg.

It has little | **speckles** |
               | spots |

all over it.
(speckle   speckles)

---

speed
speed

At what **speed** does your father drive?
How fast

It is not safe to | **speed.** |
                    | go fast. |

(speeds   sped   speeding   speeded)

---

spell
spell

Mary can **spell** the word dog.

She can put the letters in the right order
so they **spell** dog.
(spells   spelled   spelling)

I can **spend** ten cents for fruit.
pay out

Yesterday I **spent** all the money I had.
paid out

(spends   spent   spending)

spend
spend

This is a **spider** and its web.
Spiders crawl.
A **spider** has eight legs.
This is a **spider** to cook in.
skillet

(spiders)

spider
spi-der
spider

Baby **spilled the milk** on the floor.
let the milk fall

(spill   spills   spilling)

spilled
spilled

Tom has a top.
He will **spin** it.
make the top go around and around.

Spiders **spin** webs.
make

(spins   spun   spinning)

spin
spin

Spinach is a green leaf.
It is good to eat when cooked.

spinach
spin-ach
spinach

279

A B C D E F G H I J K L M N O P Q R (S) T U V W X Y Z

splash
splash

The children like to **splash** water
toss

on each other.

(splashes   splashed   splashing)

---

spoil
spoil

Do not get ink on your dress.

It will **spoil** it.

Mother put milk in the refrigerator
so it would not **spoil.**

(spoils   spoiled   spoiling)

---

spoke
spoke

Father **spoke** to Mother.
said something

(speak   speaks   speaking   spoken)

---

spoke
spoke

One **spoke** on the wheel is broken.
bar

(spokes)

---

spool
spool

This is a **spool** with thread on it.

(spools)

---

spoon
spoon

Baby eats with a **spoon.**

We eat some things with **spoons.**

Mother mixes the cake with a **spoon.**

(spoons)

Playing ball is **sport.** / fun. Games are **sports.** (sports)	**sport** *sport*
Mary got a **spot** / speck of ink on her dress. This cloth is **spotted.** / has spots on it. (spots spotted spotting)	**spot** *spot*
Mary likes to **spray** / sprinkle the flowers. (sprays sprayed spraying)	**spray** *spray*
Mother **spread** the butter on the bread. / covered the bread with butter. Mary put a bed**spread** / cover on her bed. (spreads spreading)	**spread** *spread*
These **springs** make the bed soft. The farmer plants seeds in the **spring.** Trees become green in the **spring.** (springs)	**spring** *spring*

A
B
C
D
E
F
G
H
I
J
K
L
M
N
O
P
Q
R
Ⓢ
T
U
V
W
X
Y
Z

sprinkle
sprin-kle
sprinkle

Father **sprinkles** the garden every day.

It is | **sprinkling** | today.
| raining a little |

Mother will | **sprinkle** | the clothes
| put drops of water on |

so they will iron nicely.

(sprinkles sprinkled sprinkling)

spy
spy

The children played, "I **spy**."

Someone hid a thimble.

The first to see it said, "I | **spy**."
| see." |

(spies spied spying)

square
square

This is a **square**.

All the sides are the same size.

(squares)

squash
squash

These are **squashes**.

They are red, yellow, and white.

Squashes are good to eat.

Squash pie tastes like pumpkin pie.

Sally stepped on Father's hat
and **squashed** it flat.

(squashes squashed squashing)

A
B
C
D
E
F
G
H
I
J
K
L
M
N
O
P
Q
R
Ⓢ
T
U
V
W
X
Y
Z

See Mother **squeeze** | press | the water out of the dishcloth.

squeeze
squeeze

Mary **squeezed** | pressed | the juice out of the orange.
(squeezes squeezed squeezing)

Squirrels have bushy tails.
There are red, gray, and black **squirrels**.
They like to eat nuts and grain.
(squirrel)

squirrels
squir-rels
squirrels

See the water **squirt** | rush | out of the hole in the pipe.
(squirts squirted squirting)

squirt
squirt

A **stable** is like a barn.
The farmer keeps his horses and cows in the **stable**.
(stables)

stable
sta-ble
stable

Little Bo-Peep carried a long **staff.** | pole. |
(staffs)

staff
staff

Mary is going up the **stairs.** | steps. |
(stair)

stairs
stairs

A B C D E F G H I J K L M N O P Q R S T U V W X Y Z

stake
stake

Bob tied the goat

to a **stake.**
stick pounded into the ground.

(stakes)

stalk
stalk

This is a **stalk** with corn on it.
stem

(stalks)

stamp
stamp

Father put a **stamp** on the letter.

The **stamp** shows that he paid
for sending the letter.

The horses **stamped** their feet when we came
into the stable.

(stamps   stamped   stamping)

standing
stand-ing
standing

The boy is **standing** up.

(stand   stands   stood)

stars
stars

We watched the **stars** in the sky
at night.

(star)

starch
starch

Mother put some **starch** in my dress
when she washed it.

Starch makes clothes stiff.

(starches   starched   starching)

The show will start soon.
begin

(starts   started   starting)

start
start

I live in the **state** of Michigan.

Which **state** do you live in?

There are 50 **states** in the United States.

(states)

state
state

The train stopped
at the railroad **station**.

People wait in the **station**
for trains to come and go.

We buy gasoline at a
gasoline **station**.

(stations)

station
sta-tion
station

Mother drives us to the market
in the **station wagon**.

The **station wagon** can carry many things.

(station wagons)

station wagon
sta-tion wag-on
station wagon

This is the **Statue** of Liberty.

Some **statues** are made of stone
and marble.

(statues)

statue
stat-ue
statue

Bob went to see Tom.

Mother said, **"Stay** as long as you like."

(stays   stayed   staying)

stay
stay

A B C D E F G H I J K L M N O P Q R S T U V W X Y Z

A
B
C
D
E
F
G
H
I
J
K
L
M
N
O
P
Q
R
(S)
T
U
V
W
X
Y
Z

steal
steal

The dog tried to | **steal** | the cat's supper.
take away

Stealing is taking things that do not belong to you.
(steals   stole   stealing   stolen)

steam
steam

The water in the teakettle is boiling.

See the **steam** come out.

Steam makes the engine go.

In winter **steam** gathers on the cold window glass.
(steams   steamed   steaming)

steep
steep

Bob and Mary climbed a **steep** hill.

It was almost straight up and down.
(steeper   steepest)

stem
stem

This is a flower on a **stem**. This apple has a **stem**.

The **stem** held it
to the tree.

(stems)

step
step

The baby took a long **step**.

Bob went up the | **steps.**
stairs. |

(steps   stepped   stepping)

This is a **stepladder**.

Mother stands on a **stepladder** to wash the windows.

(stepladders)

stepladder
step-lad-der
stepladder

This is a **stick** of candy.

We gathered | sticks | to make a fire.
| pieces of wood |

We use paste to | **stick** | things together.
| fasten |

(sticks   stuck   sticking   sticky)

stick
stick

A pencil is **stiff**.

It will not bend.

(stiffer   stiffest)

stiff
stiff

The baby is sleeping.

We must be | **still.** |
| quiet. |

The car is | standing **still.** |
| not moving. |

still
still

Did a bee ever **sting** you?

A **sting** is like a bite.

It hurts to be **stung** by a bee.

(stings   stung   stinging)

sting
sting

Mother | **stirs** | the cake
| mixes |

with a spoon.

(stir   stirred   stirring)

stirs
stir

A B C D E F G H I J K L M N O P Q R (S) T U V W X Y Z

stocking
stock-ing
stocking

These are silk **stockings.**
I had a hole in one **stocking.**
(stockings)

stone
stone

This is a big **stone.**
rock.

Diamonds are small **stones**
that are cut and polished.
(stones)

stood
stood

Sam sat down.

Bob **stood** up.
(stand   stands   standing)

stool
stool

A kitchen stool   A footstool   A milking stool
The farmer sits on a **stool** while milking the cows.
(stools)

stop
stop

The policeman said **stop.**

The children did not go.
(stops   stopped   stopping)

store
store

The girls wanted some candy.

They went to the **store** for it.
shop

We buy things at a **store.**
(stores)

The man who owns the store is the **storekeeper.** (storekeepers)	**storekeeper** store-keep-er *storekeeper*
The **stork** has long legs and a long bill. He can walk in deep water. (storks)	**stork** *stork*
We had a bad **storm.** Rain fell and the wind blew hard. (storms stormed storming)	**storm** *storm*
The teacher read a **story** to us. The name of the **story** was "The Three Little Pigs." (stories)	**story** sto-ry *story*
The teacher read a story from the **storybook.** (storybooks)	**storybook** sto-ry-book *storybook*
Mother cooks on this **stove.** (stoves)	**stove** *stove*

A B C D E F G H I J K L M N O P Q R (S) T U V W X Y Z

A
B
C
D
E
F
G
H
I
J
K
L
M
N
O
P
Q
R
(S)
T
U
V
W
X
Y
Z

straight
straight

This road is crooked.　　This road is **straight**.

strange
strange

A | **strange** | thing happened.
　 | queer |

(stranger　　strangest)

strap
strap

This is a shoe
without a **strap**.

This is a shoe
with a **strap**.

Father sharpened his razor on a **strap**.

Some **straps** are made of leather.

(straps)

straw
straw

Mary drank the milk through a **straw**.

A **straw** is the stem on which
grain grows.

(straws)

strawberry
straw-ber-ry
strawberry

This is a **strawberry**.

Strawberries are red.

Mother made a **strawberry** shortcake.

(strawberries)

stream
stream

This is a **stream** of water.

A **stream** is a river.

The water in the **stream** moves toward
a bigger **stream,** or a lake, or a sea.

(streams)

street
street

We drive the auto into the **street.**

Stop! Look! and Listen! before you cross the **street.**

(streets)

stretch
stretch

Rubber will **stretch** if you pull it.
get longer

Mary yawned and **stretched**
when she woke up.

(stretches   stretched   stretching)

strike
strike

Mother said, "Do not **strike** the dog."
hit

I heard the clock **strike** ten times.
sound

(strikes   striking   struck)

A B C D E F G H I J K L M N O P Q R ⓈS T U V W X Y Z

A
B
C
D
E
F
G
H
I
J
K
L
M
N
O
P
Q
R
(S)
T
U
V
W
X
Y
Z

string
string

These children can **string** beads.
put beads on a string.

The **string** is tied to the kite.
(strings   stringing   strung)

strip
strip

Mary put a **strip** of paper
long narrow piece

in her book.
(strips)

stripes
stripes

This is the American flag.

It has thirteen **stripes.**

The **stripes** are red and white.
(stripe   striped   striping)

strong
strong

Tom was so **strong** he could roll the big stone.
(stronger   strongest)

stuck
stuck

The paper had paste on it, so

it **stuck** to my book.
could not come off

(stick   sticks   sticking)

study
stud-y
study

I will **study** from a book.
read and try to learn

We study in school.
(studies   studied   studying)

Mary is making a cat of cloth for the baby.

She will **stuff** it with cotton.
fill it full of

(stuffs   stuffed   stuffing)

stuff
stuff

The bee **stung** Bob.
bit

It hurts to be **stung** by a bee.
(sting   stings   stinging)

stung
stung

If you work hard, you will **succeed.**
do well.

Father **succeeded** in starting the car.

He tried to start the car and did so.
(succeeds   succeeded   succeeding)

succeed
suc-ceed
succeed

Our baby is **such a** nice baby.
a very

We never saw **such** a storm.
a storm like that.

such
such

Suddenly it started to rain.
When we were not looking for it

Suddenly the door opened.
All at once

(sudden)

suddenly
sud-den-ly
suddenly

Candy is sweet.
It is made of **sugar.**
(sugary)

sugar
sug-ar
sugar

A
B
C
D
E
F
G
H
I
J
K
L
M
N
O
P
Q
R
Ⓢ
T
U
V
W
X
Y
Z

suggestion
sug-ges-tion
suggestion

Bob wanted to make a box.

Father said, "Maybe I can give you

a **suggestion** about making it."
an idea

Perhaps Father's **suggestion** will work.
plan

(suggestions)

suit
suit

Father has on a dark **suit.**

The teacher liked Mary's pictures

and said, "They **suit** me."
please

(suits   suited   suiting)

summer
sum-mer
summer

The snow falls in winter.

The flowers grow in **summer.**

It is very warm in **summer.**

(summers)

sun
sun

The **sun** is in the sky.

We see the **sun** in the daytime.

The **sun** makes us warm.

(suns   sunny)

Sunday
Sun-day
Sunday

We do not go to school on **Sunday.**

Sunday is the first day of the week.

The **sunflower** is tall. The center is brown. The outside is yellow. Birds like the seeds from a **sunflower.** (sunflowers)	**sunflower** sun-flow-er *sunflower*
At night there is no **sunlight.** light from the sun.	**sunlight** sun-light *sunlight*
The **sunrise** was pretty today. coming up of the sun (sunrises)	**sunrise** sun-rise *sunrise*
In the evening we watched the **sunset.** going down of the sun. (sunsets)	**sunset** sun-set *sunset*
The **sunshine** sunlight came through the window.	**sunshine** sun-shine *sunshine*
In the morning we eat breakfast. At night we eat **supper.**	**supper** sup-per *supper*

A
B
C
D
E
F
G
H
I
J
K
L
M
N
O
P
Q
R
(S)
T
U
V
W
X
Y
Z

suppose
sup-pose
suppose

I | suppose / think | I can go to the party.

(supposes   supposed   supposing)

sure
sure

Jack was **sure** that his mother
would let him go to the party.
(surely)

surprise
sur-prise
surprise

Mary had a birthday party.

We are having a **surprise** party for her.

Mary does not know about the party.
(surprises   surprised   surprising)

swallow
swal-low
swallow

The boy put too much bread into his mouth
at one time.

He could not **swallow** it.

This bird is a **swallow.**

Some **swallows** build nests in barns.

Some build nests in the sides of hills.
(swallows   swallowing   swallowed)

swam
swam

This boy **swam** across the river.
(swim   swims   swimming   swum)

sweater
sweat-er
sweater

This is a **sweater** to wear.

It will keep you warm.
(sweaters)

Mother can **sweep** the floor clean with a broom.

(sweeps   sweeping   swept)

sweep
sweep

This man is a street **sweeper.**

He sweeps the streets clean.

(sweepers)

sweeper
sweep-er
sweeper

Candy is **sweet.**
not sour.

(sweeter   sweetest   sweetly)

(sweeten   sweetens   sweetened   sweetening)

sweet
sweet

Baby bumped her arm.

Her arm began to **swell.**
get larger.

(swells   swelled   swelling   swollen)

swell
swell

The boy is **swift** with his work.
fast

The dog runs **swiftly.**

(swifter   swiftest   swiftly)

swift
swift

See this boy **swim** in the water.

Fish **swim** in the water, too.

(swims   swam   swimming   swum)

swim
swim

A
B
C
D
E
F
G
H
I
J
K
L
M
N
O
P
Q
R
Ⓢ
T
U
V
W
X
Y
Z

swing
swing

This is a **swing**.

Mary **swings** in the **swing**.

It goes back and forth.

(swings   swinging   swung)

sword
sword

This **sword** has sharp edges.

Men used to fight with **swords**.

(swords)

syrup
syr-up
syrup

Syrup is made with sugar and water or juices.

Do you like maple **syrup** on pancakes
for your breakfast?

This is a table.

We sit at a table when we eat.

(tables)

table
ta-ble
table

Mary is writing in her **tablet.**
| book of paper. |

Some medicine is round pills
and some is flat **tablets.**

(tablets)

tablet
tab-let
tablet

The man put a **tag** on the dog's collar.

The **tag** had the dog's name on it.

The children played **tag.**

Bob | **tagged** | Tom, then Tom
| touched |

chased the other children.

(tags   tagged   tagging)

tag
tag

The horse has a long **tail.**

The rabbit has a short **tail.**

(tails)

tail
tail

The man who makes Father's clothes
is called a **tailor.**

(tailors)

tailor
tai-lor
tailor

A B C D E F G H I J K L M N O P Q R S T U V W X Y Z

A
B
C
D
E
F
G
H
I
J
K
L
M
N
O
P
Q
R
S
Ⓣ
U
V
W
X
Y
Z

take *take*	Mother said she would take us for a ride. / go with Bob **takes** Father's hand when they cross **the street.** (**takes** took **taking** **taken**)
tale *tale*	Our teacher told us a tale. / story. (tales)
talk *talk*	Bob wanted to **talk.** / say something. (talks talking talked)
tall *tall*	One girl is short. The other is **tall.** (taller tallest)
tame *tame*	Dogs and cats are tame animals. / not wild It is possible to **tame** some wild animals. (tames tamed)
tan *tan*	Jane's hat is a tan color. / light brown
tangle tan-gle *tangle*	Mary's hair gets tangled at night. / twisted together Does your hair **tangle** when you sleep? (tangles tangled tangling)

This is a **tank**
for hot water.

The soldiers fight
with this **tank.**

Father put gasoline in the **tank** of our automobile.
(tanks)

tank
tank

We heard a | **tap** | on the window.
| light knock |

I **tapped** on Mother's door.

The water runs out of the **tap**
into the sink.
(taps   tapped   tapping)

tap
tap

Mary has never been | **tardy** | for school.
| late |

(tardier   tardiest)

tardy
tar-dy
tardy

A **tart** is a small pie
with jelly or jam in it.
(tarts)

tart
tart

This is a hat
with a **tassel** on it.

Stalks of corn
have **tassels,** too.
(tassels)

tassel
tas-sel
tassel

A B C D E F G H I J K L M N O P Q R S (T) U V W X Y Z

taste
taste

Baby put the candy in her mouth.

She liked the sweet **taste** of it.

Mother let Mary **taste** the ice cream.

(tastes   tasted   tasting)

taught
taught

Bob's father **taught him** to skate.
helped him learn

(teach   teaches   teaching)

tax
tax

We pay **taxes** to the city.
money

Tax money is used to pay policemen, firemen, and other helpers.

(taxes   taxed   taxing)

tea
tea

Children drink milk.

Mother and Father drink **tea.**

Tea is made from dried **tea** leaves.

teach
teach

Can you make a kite?

I will **teach you** how.
help you learn

(teaches   taught   teaching)

teacher
teach-er
teacher

We go to school.

Our **teacher** helps us learn to read.

(teachers)

302

Our school has a baseball **team.**

A baseball **team** is nine boys
who play ball together.

(teams)

team
team

Jane will **tear** the paper in two.

Mother said, "Do not | **tear** | your dress."
| make a hole in |

(tears   tore   tearing   torn)

tear
tear

Mary is crying.

She has | **tears** | in her eyes.
| drops of water |

(tear)

tears
tears

A teaspoon is a small spoon.

We eat ice cream with a **teaspoon.**

(teaspoons   teaspoonful)

teaspoon
tea-spoon
teaspoon

This is the baby's toy **Teddy bear.**

She likes to play with it.

(Teddy bears)

Teddy bear
Ted-dy bear
Teddy bear

Baby opened his mouth.

He had two white **teeth.**

(tooth)

teeth
teeth

A B C D E F G H I J K L M N O P Q R S (T) U V W X Y Z

telegram
tel-e-gram
telegram

Harry had a telegram message from Father.

(telegrams)

telephone
tel-e-phone
telephone

Bob and Mary are talking over the **telephone.**

(telephones)

television
tel-e-vi-sion
television

It's nice to have a **television.** There are many **television** programs just for children.

(televisions)

tell
tell

The children asked the teacher to **tell** a story.

(tells   telling   told)

ten
ten

Do you see ten stars?
10

10

(tenth)

Some meat is tough and hard to chew.

Some meat is | **tender** | and easy to chew.
         soft

(tenderer   tenderest   tenderly)

tender
ten-der
tender

This is a **tent.**

It is fun to live in a **tent**
in summer.
(tents)

tent
tent

Mother had a | **terrible** | cold.
        very bad

(terribly)

terrible
ter-ri-ble
terrible

This dog is a **terrier.**
(terriers)

terrier
ter-ri-er
terrier

Our teacher gave us a **test**
to see how well we could read.
(tests)

test
test

Bob is bigger **than** Jane.

than
than

The woman gave me an apple.
I said, **"Thank** you."
(thanks   thanking   thanked   thankful)

thank
thank

A B C D E F G H I J K L M N O P Q R S (T) U V W X Y Z

Thanksgiving
Thanks-giv-ing
Thanksgiving

On **Thanksgiving** Day
we say thanks to God
for all He has done for us.

that
that

Mary wants this book,
and I want **that** one over there.

that's
that's

That's / That is the last apple I have.

the
the

This story is about **the** three bears.

their
their

Three little kittens
Lost **their** mittens.
(theirs)

them
them

The goats were in the turnip field.

"One, two, I will get **them** out for you,"
said the wolf.

themselves
them-selves
themselves

The girls kept the apples for **themselves**.

then
then

"I will come to the party **then."** / **at that time."**

there
there

Father said,

"Put the book **there."** / **in that place."**

306

It is late; **therefore,** we can't go. *for that reason,*	**therefore** there-fore *therefore*
There's one more flower in bloom. There is	**there's** *there's*
This book is mine. **These** books are mine, too.	**these** *these*
The children were running. **They** are very tired.	**they** *they*
They're going to the party. They are	**they're** *they're*
Baby has much hair. Her hair is **thick.** This book is thin. (thicker | This one is **thick.** thickest)	**thick** *thick*
A **thief** is a person who takes things that do not belong to him. (thieves)	**thief** *thief*
Mother puts this **thimble** on her finger when she sews. (thimbles)	**thimble** thim-ble *thimble*

A
B
C
D
E
F
G
H
I
J
K
L
M
N
O
P
Q
R
S
(T)
U
V
W
X
Y
Z

thin
thin

This book is **thin.** not thick.

This boy is **thin.** not fat.

(thinner   thinnest)

thing
thing

Baby puts **things** in her mouth.

Mary didn't have a **thing** to play with.

(things)

think
think

I **think** it is colder today.
believe

When we are away, Mother **thinks** of us all the time.

(thinks   thinking   thought)

third
third

Mary is the **third** child from the end of the row.
She is number three in the row.

(thirds)

thirsty
thirst-y
thirsty

Billy drank some water.

He was **thirsty.**

(thirstier   thirstiest)

thirteen
thir-teen
thirteen

Ten apples and three apples make

thirteen apples.
13

13

ten, 10	twenty, 20	thirty 30	**30**	**thirty** thir-ty *thirty*

Thirty cents is a quarter and a nickel.

Twenty marbles and fifteen marbles
make **thirty-five** marbles.
35

thirty-five
thir-ty-five
thirtyfive

That book is mine.
This one is yours.

this
this

This plant is a **thistle.**

Some **thistles** have purple flowers.

The **thistles** have sharp stickers
    on the stems.
            (thistles)

thistle
this-tle
thistle

Some plants have **thorns** on them.
sharp points

Roses have **thorns.**

Thorns will stick you.
    (thorn)

thorns
thorns

These books are mine.
Those books over there are yours.

those
those

A B C D E F G H I J K L M N O P Q R S T U V W X Y Z

though
though

Bob went to the party even **though** it was late.

It was late, but he went anyway.

thought
thought

I | **thought** | I could go.
| believed |

The things you think about are your **thoughts.**

(think   thinks   thinking   thoughts)

thread
thread

This is a spool of **thread.**

We sew our clothes with **thread.**

Watch Grandma | **thread** | her needle.
| put thread through |

(threads   threading   threaded)

three
three

Here are | **three** | stars.
| 3 |

☆ ☆ ☆   3

thresh
thresh

Did you ever see a farmer

| **thresh** | wheat?
| take the seeds from |

(threshes   threshed   threshing)

throat
throat

The boy has his hand

on | his **throat.**
| the front of his neck. |

(throats)

This is the **throne** | seat |
where the king or queen sits.
(thrones)

throne
throne

Father looked **through** the book for a picture.

I put the thread **through** the eye of the needle.

We went **through** the tunnel.

We are **through** | finished | with our work.

through
through

See Jack **throw** the ball.
(throws   threw   throwing   thrown)

throw
throw

This hand has four fingers and one **thumb.**
(thumbs)

thumb
thumb

The man **thumped** | pounded | the drum.

(thump   thumps   thumping)

thumped
thumped

I saw the lightning and heard the **thunder** when it rained.
(thunders   thundered   thundering)

thunder
thun-der
thunder

A B C D E F G H I J K L M N O P Q R S **T** U V W X Y Z

Thursday
Thurs-day
Thursday

Thursday is the fifth day of the week.

tick
tick

The clock says, **tick,** tock.
(ticks   ticked   ticking)

ticket
tick-et
ticket

Bob gave the conductor his **ticket.**

He paid money for the **ticket.**

The conductor will let him ride
if he has a **ticket.**
(tickets)

tickled
tick-led
tickled

The dog licked my hand with his tongue.

It **tickled** my hand.
made shivery little feelings on

I was **tickled** to get new shoes.
pleased
(tickle   tickles   tickling)

tidy
ti-dy
tidy

Mother is very **tidy.**
neat.

She puts things where they belong.
(tidier   tidiest)

tie
tie

This is Father's **tie.**

Billy tried to **tie** fasten
the strings together.

Father **tied** the dog to the post.
(ties   tying   tied)

This is a **tiger**. His fur has yellow and black stripes. **Tigers** are wild. (tigers)	**tiger** ti-ger *tiger*
The ring is **tight** on my finger. not loose (tighter tightest tightly)	**tight** *tight*
He ran **till** he saw a fox. until	**till** *till*
The **time** was ten o'clock. Once upon a **time** I saw a bear. (times)	**time** *time*
She put the gingerbread boy in a **tin** pan to bake. Mother bought a **tin** can of corn.	**tin** *tin*
Hear the **tinkle** of the bells. sound (tinkles tinkled tinkling)	**tinkle** tin-kle *tinkle*
The baby is **tiny.** very small. (tinier tiniest)	**tiny** ti-ny *tiny*
Baby **tipped** over the glass of milk. upset (tip tips tipping)	**tipped** *tipped*

A B C D E F G H I J K L M N O P Q R S (T) U V W X Y Z

tiptoes
tip-toes
tiptoes

Baby is standing

on | her **tiptoes.**
the ends of her toes.

(tiptoe)

tire
tire

Father put a new **tire**
on the car.

Hard work will | **tire** you.
make you tired.

(tires   tired   tiring)

tired
tired

I worked hard.

I am too **tired** to play.

(tire   tires   tiring)

title
ti-tle
title

What is the | **title** | of the story you are reading?
name

The **title** of this book is
"The Picture Dictionary for Children."

(titles)

to
to

Jack threw the ball | **to** Mary.
in Mary's direction.

Mary likes **to** help Mother.

toad
toad

This is a **toad.**

He looks like a frog.

He has no tail.

He eats bugs and worms.

(toads)

I eat **toasted** bread for breakfast.

We make **toast** in a toaster.

I like brown **toast**.

(toasts   toasted   toasting)

toast
toast

Father smokes **tobacco** in his pipe.

tobacco
to-bac-co
tobacco

I am going to school today.
on this day.

today
to-day
today

We have five **toes** on each foot.

(toe)

toes
toes

The children sat together.
with each other.

together
to-geth-er
together

Bob could not read to us so he **told** us a story.

Father **told** Mary she could go.

(tell   tells   telling)

told
told

This is a **tomato**.

Tomatoes grow on vines.

Tomatoes are red.

They are good to eat.

(tomatoes)

tomato
to-ma-to
tomato

A
B
C
D
E
F
G
H
I
J
K
L
M
N
O
P
Q
R
S
(T)
U
V
W
X
Y
Z

tomorrow to-mor-row *tomorrow*	I am going to school **tomorrow.** one day after today.
ton *ton*	Father bought a **ton** of coal. There are 2,000 pounds in a **ton.** (tons)
tongue *tongue*	The dog's mouth is open. We can see his **tongue.** Our **tongues** are in our mouths. You could not talk if you had no **tongue.** (tongues)
tonight to-night *tonight*	You can see the stars if you look into the sky **tonight.** this evening.
too *too*	Father went to the store. Bob went to the store, **too.** also. This box is **too** heavy for Bob to lift. It is so heavy that he cannot lift it.
took *took*	The cow wanted a drink. Bob **took** some water to her. carried (take takes taking taken)

tools
tools

When a man makes a house, he uses these **tools.**

A **tool** is anything you use when you work.

(tool)

tooth
tooth

When Baby opened her mouth,
    I saw one **tooth.**
        (teeth)

toothache
tooth-ache
toothache

Did you ever have a | **toothache?**
                      pain in a tooth? |

toothbrush
tooth-brush
toothbrush

This is a **toothbrush.**
We clean our teeth with a **toothbrush.**
        (toothbrushes)

top
top

Bob likes to spin his **top.**

The roof is the **top** of the house.

        Mother put the can on the | **top** | shelf.
                                    highest

            (tops)

torn
torn

Mary and Spot were playing.

Her dress was **torn** by the dog.
(tear   tears   tore   tearing)

A B C D E F G H I J K L M N O P Q R S T U V W X Y Z

A
B
C
D
E
F
G
H
I
J
K
L
M
N
O
P
Q
R
S
(T)
U
V
W
X
Y
Z

tortoise
tor-toise
tortoise

This is a **tortoise.**

We call him a turtle.

He has a shell on his back.

He lives on land.

(tortoises)

toss
toss

The boys like

to **toss** the ball up in the air.
throw

(tosses   tossing   tossed)

touch
touch

See Baby **touch** the wall.
put his hand against

(touches   touching   touched)

tough
tough

Some meat is tender and some meat is **tough.**

Tough meat is hard to chew.

(tougher   toughest)

toward
to-ward
toward

The auto is going **toward** the hills.
in the direction of

(towards)

towel
tow-el
towel

This is a bath **towel.**

Mary wiped her face dry
on a clean **towel.**

(towels)

Some children live in the country.

We live in a **town.**
place where many people live.
(towns)

town
town

Santa Claus brought many **toys.**
playthings.

I like to play with **toys.**
(toy)

toys
toys

This is a **track** for a train.

We saw a rabbit's **tracks**
footprints

in the snow.
(tracks)

track
track

Mary and Betty will **trade** papers.
exchange

My father's **trade** is building houses.
business

He is a carpenter by **trade.**
(trades   traded   trading)

trade
trade

There is much **traffic** today.
Many trucks and cars are going by.

traffic
traf-fic
traffic

A B C D E F G H I J K L M N O P Q R S Ⓣ U V W X Y Z

319

trailer
trail-er
trailer

Many people live
in a **trailer**
in summer.

Men use this **trailer**
to move things
from place to place.

(trailers)

train
train

The **train** is on the track.

This **train** carries people and mail.

(trains)

tramp
tramp

The man has no home.

He walks from town to town.

He is a **tramp.**

The cows | **tramped** | on the flowers.
         | walked |

(tramps   tramped   tramping)

traps
traps

We catch mice and rats in **traps.**

(trap)

We like to **travel.**
go from place to place.

We **travel** in our autos.
go

Some people **travel** on the train.

(travels   traveled   traveling)

travel
trav-el
travel

A **traveler** is a person who is going
from one place to another.

(travelers)

traveler
trav-el-er
traveler

Father's dinner is
on the **tray.**

(trays)

tray
tray

The children **treat** Mother kindly.
act toward

Bob **treated** Tom to an ice-cream cone.
gave Tom

(treats   treated   treating)

treat
treat

This is a **tree.**

Most **trees** lose their leaves
in the winter.

The pine **tree** is green all the time.

(trees)

tree
tree

A B C D E F G H I J K L M N O P Q R S T U V W X Y Z

trembled trem-bled *trembled*	The dog was so cold that he **trembled.** / shook all over. (tremble trembles trembling)
trial tri-al *trial*	Father is giving his new car a **trial.** / try out.
triangles tri-ang-les *triangles*	These are **triangles.** They all have three sides. (triangle)
tribe *tribe*	The Indian was the chief of his **tribe.** / group. (tribes)
tricks *tricks*	Bob's dog can stand up and beg. He can do other **tricks,** too. (trick)
tricycle tri-cy-cle *tricycle*	A **tricycle** has three wheels. (tricycles)
tried *tried*	The jam was on the shelf. Bob **tried** to reach it. (try tries trying)

See the children **trim** the Christmas tree.

They are putting colored balls **on it.**

Mary's new dress is **trimmed** with buttons.

(trims   trimmed   trimming)

trim
trim

Baby **tripped** on the rug and fell.
caught her foot

Be careful not to **trip** on the rug.

We went for a long **trip** in the car.
journey

(trips   tripped   tripping)

trip
trip

It isn't any **trouble** to stop for you.
extra work

Bad boys get into **trouble.**

Some children make **trouble** for their mother.

(troubles   troubled   troubling)

trouble
trou-ble
trouble

Father has on dark **trousers.**
pants.

trousers
trou-sers
trousers

A
B
C
D
E
F
G
H
I
J
K
L
M
N
O
P
Q
R
S
(T)
U
V
W
X
Y
Z

A
B
C
D
E
F
G
H
I
J
K
L
M
N
O
P
Q
R
S
(T)
U
V
W
X
Y
Z

truck
truck

This is a big **truck.**

Trucks carry heavy loads.

(trucks)

true
true

The story is not | **true.**
| correct.

(truer   truest   truly)

trunk
trunk

We put our clothes in the **trunk.**

Elephants have long **trunks.**

(trunks)

trust
trust

I | **trust** | Bob, because he tells the truth.
| believe |

(trusts   trusted   trusting)

truth
truth

Tom told | the **truth.**
| what was right.

It pays to tell the **truth.**

(truthful   truthfully)

try
try

If you | **try hard** | you will get the picture finished.
| do your best |

(tries   tried   trying)

tub
tub

A **tub** will hold water.

(tubs)

This is a **tube** of toothpaste.
(tubes)

tube
tube

The third day of the week is **Tuesday.**

Tuesday
Tues-day
Tuesday

These flowers are **tulips.**
They are of many bright colors.
(tulips)

tulip
tu-lip
tulip

Clowns | **tumble** / roll | on the grass.

The baby | **tumbled** / fell | off the bed.

(tumbles   tumbled   tumbling)

tumble
tum-ble
tumble

This is a glass **tumbler.**
We drink from a **tumbler.**
(tumblers)

tumbler
tum-bler
tumbler

Men dig | **tunnels.** / ways through hills. |

Trains go through **tunnels.**
(tunnel)

tunnels
tun-nels
tunnels

This is a **turkey.**
Turkeys are good to eat.
(turkeys)

turkey
tur-key
turkey

A B C D E F G H I J K L M N O P Q R S (T) U V W X Y Z

turn
turn

We can't all get a drink at **once**.

We wait our **turn**.

The car **turned** the corner.
(turns   turned   turning)

turnip
tur-nip
turnip

This is a **turnip**.

Turnips grow in the ground.

Turnips are good to eat.
(turnips)

turtle
tur-tle
turtle

The **turtle** has a shell on his back.

He swims in the water.
(turtles)

tusks
tusks

The elephant has two **tusks.**
outside teeth.

(tusk)

twelve
twelve

☆☆☆☆☆☆☆☆☆☆☆☆

Here are **twelve** stars.

Count them.
(twelfth)

12

twenty
twen-ty
twenty

1 2 3 4 5 6 7 8 9 10 11 12 13 14 15 16 17 18 19 20

These are numbers from one to **twenty.**
20.

20

Mother called Mary twice.
two times.

twice
twice

The boys gathered twigs to make a fire.
small branches from trees
(twig)

twigs
twigs

These boys are **twins.**

They are brothers.

They were born on the same day.
(twin)

twins
twins

See the stars **twinkle.**

Sometimes they are very bright and
sometimes they are not.
(twinkles   twinkled   twinkling)

twinkle
twin-kle
twinkle

The wires are twisted together.
wound
(twist   twists   twisting)

twisted
twist-ed
twisted

How many stars do you see?

I see **two** stars.
(two's)

2

two
two

This is a **typewriter.**

We can write on a **typewriter.**
(typewriters)

typewriter
type-writ-er
typewriter

A B C D E F G H I J K L M N O P Q R S (T) U V W X Y Z

A
B
C
D
E
F
G
H
I
J
K
L
M
N
O
P
Q
R
S
T
(U)
V
W
X
Y
Z

ugly
ug-ly
ugly

The witch that the fairy saw

was **ugly.**
not nice to look at.

Our teacher read the story of the **Ugly** Duckling.
(uglier   ugliest)

umbrella
um-brel-la
umbrella

Mary's **umbrella**
keeps the rain off Mary.
(umbrellas)

uncle
un-cle
uncle

The man is Father's brother.

He is my **uncle.**
(uncles)

under
un-der
under

The dish is on the table.

The shoes are **under** the table.

underneath
un-der-neath
underneath

The shoes are **underneath** the table.
under

understand
un-der-stand

understand

Baby does not talk plainly.

It is hard to **understand** her.
tell what she is saying.

I don't **understand** how to spell.
know

I do not **understand** you.
know what you mean.

(understands   understood   understanding)

We wear **underwear** to keep us warm. underclothes	**underwear** un-der-wear *underwear*
Watch Mother **undress** the baby. take off the baby's clothes. (undresses undressed undressing)	**undress** un-dress *undress*
Mary **unfolded** her handkerchief. opened out (unfold unfolds unfolding)	**unfolded** un-fold-ed *unfolded*
When Tom is bad, Mother is **unhappy.** sad. (unhappily)	**unhappy** un-hap-py *unhappy*
We are Americans. We live in the **United States.**	**United States** U-nit-ed States *United States*
Some boys are **unkind** to their dogs. not kind	**unkind** un-kind *unkind*
The name of the man is **unknown.** not known.	**unknown** un-known *unknown*

A B C D E F G H I J K L M N O P Q R S T Ⓤ V W X Y Z

unless
un-less
unless

You need not go **unless you** want to.
if you do not

untie
un-tie
untie

Mary tied her ribbon in a knot.

She pulled one end of the ribbon
to **untie** the bow.

(unties   untying   untied)

until
un-til
until

Bob came for me.

I was not ready **to go until** I washed
my face and hands.

up
up

One kite is high **up** in the sky.
above

The other is down on the ground.

Jack and Jill
Went **up** the hill.

upon
up-on
upon

Mother set the dish **upon** the table.
on

upper
up-per
upper

Mary's name is in

the **upper** right corner of the paper.
higher

See Jane go upstairs to bed.
up the stairs

Her room is **upstairs.**

upstairs
up-stairs
upstairs

The children looked **upward.**
above.

upward
up-ward
upward

We are going to the party.

Will you go with **us?**

us
us

Mary did not have a book.

"You may **use** mine," said Bob.
(uses   using   used)

use
use

A hammer is **useful.**

It can be used for many things.

useful
use-ful
useful

A B C D E F G H I J K L M N O P Q R S T Ⓤ V W X Y Z

vacation
va-ca-tion
vacation

When school is out,

we are going to have a **vacation.**
time for play and rest.

(vacations)

---

valentine
val-en-tine
valentine

This is a **valentine.**

St. Valentine's Day is on February 14.

(valentines)

---

valuable
val-u-a-ble
valuable

Mother's diamond ring is **valuable.**
worth much money.

---

value
val-ue
value

What is the **value** of Mother's ring?
price

How much is it worth?

(values valued valuing)

---

van
van

This is a moving **van.**

Men move furniture in moving **vans.**

(vans)

---

vase
vase

The flowers are in a **vase.**

(vases)

vegetable
veg-e-ta-ble
vegetable

Corn, potatoes, cabbage, and carrots
   are **vegetables.**

We eat **vegetables** to keep us well.

Do you know other **vegetables?**

(vegetables)

velvet
vel-vet
velvet

Velvet is a soft silk cloth.

Dresses are made of **velvet.**

verse
verse

Bob knows only one | **verse** | of the poem.
                    | line |

(verses)

very
ver-y
very

It is a **very** warm day.

Dick is a **very** small boy.

vest
vest

A **vest** has no sleeves.

Father wears a **vest** under his coat.

(vests)

A B C D E F G H I J K L M N O P Q R S T U (V) W X Y Z

view
view

We saw a beautiful | **view** | of the river.
| scene |

We | **viewed** | the river from the train.
| saw |

(views   viewed   viewing)

village
vil-lage
village

A **village** is a small group of houses.

Towns are bigger than **villages.**

(villages)

vine
vine

Grapes grow on a **vine.**

Watermelons grow on **vines,** too.

Some flowers grow on **vines.**

(vines)

vinegar
vin-e-gar
vinegar

Mother puts **vinegar** on pickles.

Vinegar makes the pickles sour.

violet
vi-o-let
violet

This flower is a **violet.**

Violets are purple, yellow, or white.

(violets)

This is a **violin**. I like the music of a **violin**. (violins)	**violin** vi-o-lin *violin*
We are going to **visit** / see our aunt. (visits visiting visited)	**visit** vis-it *visit*
Several **visitors** / people came to see us. (visitors)	**visitor** vis-i-tor *visitor*
When you talk or sing, a sound comes through your mouth. This sound is your **voice**. (voices)	**voice** *voice*
I wanted Bob for our captain, so I **voted** for him. Bob had fifteen **votes**. (vote voted voting)	**votes** *votes*
Father is going on a long **voyage**. / trip across the sea. He is going on a big boat. (voyages)	**voyage** voy-age *voyage*

A
B
C
D
E
F
G
H
I
J
K
L
M
N
O
P
Q
R
S
T
U
(V)
W
X
Y
Z

wade
wade

Children like to | **wade** | in the water.
| walk |

(wades waded wading)

---

wag
wag

My dog likes me.

See him | **wag** his tail.
| move his tail from side to side.

(wags wagged wagging)

---

wages
wag-es
wages

Father's | **wages** are | $100.00 a week.
| pay is |

We work to earn our | **wages.**
| money. |

(wage)

---

wagon
wag-on
wagon

See Bob take the baby for a ride in his **wagon.**

(wagons)

---

waist
waist

Bob put his belt around his **waist.**

(waists)

---

wait
wait

The door was not open.

I had to **wait** for someone to open it.

The groceryman said, "May I | **wait** on | you?"
| serve |

(waits waited waiting)

This man is **a waiter**. He waits on us. He puts food on the table for us to eat. (waiters)	**waiter** wait-er *waiter*
Little Boy Blue is fast asleep. Will you **wake** him? (wakes waked waking woke)	**wake** *wake*
Bob is not running. He is **walking**. Will you **walk** with me? Do not play in the street. Play on the side**walk**. (walks walked walking)	**walk** *walk*
Mother hung the picture on the **wall**. (walls)	**wall** *wall*
The man put the **wallpaper** on the wall.	**wallpaper** wall-pa-per *wallpaper*
Walnuts grow on trees. They are good to eat. Some furniture is made from the wood of **walnut** trees. (walnuts)	**walnut** wal-nut *walnut*

A
B
C
D
E
F
G
H
I
J
K
L
M
N
O
P
Q
R
S
T
U
V
W
X
Y
Z

A
B
C
D
E
F
G
H
I
J
K
L
M
N
O
P
Q
R
S
T
U
V
(W)
X
Y
Z

walrus
wal-rus
walrus

This animal is a **walrus.**
He lives in the water.
See his long tusks.

wander
wan-der
wander

Bob and his dog liked to
| **wander** through the woods. |
| walk slowly |

(wanders   wandered   wandering)

want
want

Baby saw Tom's cookies.
She **wanted** some, too.
I | **want** one, too. |
| should like to have |

(wants   wanted   wanting)

war
war

The soldiers went to **war**
to fight for their country.
(wars)

warm
warm

The sun makes us **warm.**
The snow makes us cold.
(warmer   warmest)

warned
warned

Before we started to school,
Mother | **warned** us about | crossing the street |
| told us of the danger of |
when the light was red.
(warns   warn   warning)

There **was** an old woman,

Who lived in a shoe.

It **was** raining when I came home.

was
was

Mary is **washing** her face.

Mary likes to **wash** her face.

Mother **washes** our clothes on Monday.

(washes   washed   washing)

wash
wash

This is a **washbowl.**

We wash our hands in the **washbowl.**

(washbowls)

washbowl
wash-bowl
washbowl

We use a **washcloth** in the
bath or shower.

(wash-cloths)

washcloth
wash-cloth
washcloth

This is a **washing machine.**

We wash clothes in a **washing machine.**

(washing machines)

washing machine
wash-ing ma-chine
washing machine

This is a picture
of George **Washington.**

He was the first president of the United States.

Washington
Wash-ing-ton
Washington

A
B
C
D
E
F
G
H
I
J
K
L
M
N
O
P
Q
R
S
T
U
V
Ⓦ
X
Y
Z

wasn't
wasnt

It **wasn't** very warm today.
| was not |

wasp
wasp

This is a **wasp.**

It stings like a bee.

(wasps)

waste
waste

We put paper that has been used in the **waste** basket.

The boy **wastes** his paste.
| uses more paste than he needs. |

(wastes   wasted   wasting   wasteful)

watch
watch

This is Grandpa's watch.

He will tell you what time it is by his **watch.**

Mary likes to **watch** the baby.
| look after |

I like to **watch** the men building the house.
| look at |

(watches   watched   watching)

water
wa-ter
water

We drink **water.**

Mother filled the pitcher with **water.**

Bob **watered** the flowers.
| put water on |

Boats sail on **water.**

(waters   watered   watering)

The **water lily** grows in the water.

Its flat leaves float on the top
  of the water.

(water lilies)

water lily
wa-ter lil-y
water lily

This is a **watermelon.**

It is red inside
  and green outside.

Watermelons grow on a vine.

The vine is on the ground.

Watermelons are good to eat.

(watermelons)

watermelon
wa-ter-mel-on
watermelon

Mother has a **wave** in her hair.

See Father **wave** his hand at the children.

Can you see the **waves**
  in the water?

(waves   waved   waving)

wave
wave

Some candles are made of **wax.**

Father **waxed** the floors.
put wax on

It made them smooth.

(waxes   waxed   waxing)

wax
wax

A
B
C
D
E
F
G
H
I
J
K
L
M
N
O
P
Q
R
S
T
U
V
W
X
Y
Z

A
B
C
D
E
F
G
H
I
J
K
L
M
N
O
P
Q
R
S
T
U
V
W
X
Y
Z

way
way

Mary did not know which **way** to go.

Bob said, "I will show you the **way."** road."

This is the **way** how we wash our clothes.

(ways)

we
we

We will go.
You and I

We will go.
The children and I

weak
weak

Baby cannot lift the jar.

She is too **weak.** not strong enough.

(weaker   weakest   weakly)

wear
wear

Betty put on her new dress.

She likes to **wear** her new dress.
(wears   wore   wearing   worn)

weary
wea-ry
weary

We played so hard that we were **weary.** tired.

weather
weath-er
weather

Sometimes it is warm and sometimes it is cold.

I like warm **weather** best.

I do not like rainy **weather.**

I like sunshiny **weather.**

See the Indian **weave** the rug.
She goes under and over,
   under and over each thread.
(weaves   wove   weaving)

weave
weave

This is a spider's **web.**
The spider spins his own **web.**
He catches flies in his **web.**
(webs)

web
web

The feet of a goose are **webbed.**
The toes are fastened together
   with a web of skin.
Webbed feet help geese to swim.

webbed
webbed

Father and Mother were | **wed** | a long time ago.
                          | married |

wed
wed

The fourth day of the week is **Wednesday.**
Monday, Tuesday, **Wednesday.**
2nd day, 3rd day, 4th day.

Wednesday
Wednes-day
Wednesday

I have a | **wee** | kitten.
          | very little |

wee
wee

Some plants grow where they are not wanted.
These plants are **weeds.**
Dandelions are **weeds.**

In the summer we | **weed** | our garden.
                  | pull the weeds out of |

(weeds   weeded   weeding)

weed
weed

A B C D E F G H I J K L M N O P Q R S T U V W X Y Z

A
B
C
D
E
F
G
H
I
J
K
L
M
N
O
P
Q
R
S
T
U
V
(W)
X
Y
Z

week *week*	There are seven days **in a week.** Monday, Tuesday, Wednesday, Thursday, Friday, Saturday, and Sunday are the days of the **week.** (weeks)
weep *weep*	Mary broke her doll. She started to **weep.** cry. (weeps wept weeping)
weighs *weighs*	Bob is seeing how much he **weighs.** heavy he is. He **weighs** 40 pounds. (weigh weighed weighing)
welcome wel-come *welcome*	Mary thanked Bob for the book. Bob said, "You are **welcome.**" We are **welcome** at Grandma's. She is always glad to see us. (welcomes welcomed welcoming)
well *well*	I am **well.** not sick. A **well** is a deep hole in the ground with good water in it.
we'll *we'll*	**We'll** play with you. We will

Mary asked me to go to her party, so I **went** to it.	**went** *went*
Mary **wept** / cried when she broke her doll. (weep weeps weeping)	**wept** *wept*
The ponies **were** glad to have their oats.	**were** *were*
We're / We are making a kite.	**we're** *we're*
The sun comes up in the east. The sun goes down in the **west**. (western)	**west** *west*
Water makes the grass **wet**. The sunshine makes the grass dry. (wets wetting)	**wet** *wet*
This big animal is a **whale**. He lives in the sea. (whales)	**whale** *whale*
There was an old woman Who lived in a shoe. She had so many children She didn't know **what** to do. **What** are you making?	**what** *what*

A B C D E F G H I J K L M N O P Q R S T U V W X Y Z

A
B
C
D
E
F
G
H
I
J
K
L
M
N
O
P
Q
R
S
T
U
V
(W)
X
Y
Z

what's
what's

My name is John.

What's your name?
What is

wheat
wheat

This is **wheat.**

Wheat is a grain.

We make flour from **wheat.**

Bread is made from flour.

wheels
wheel

The wagon has four **wheels.**

The **wheels** are round.

The **wheels** have spokes
to make them strong.
(wheel)

wheelbarrow
wheel-bar-row
wheelbarrow

A wheelbarrow
(wheelbarrows)

when
when

We are going for a ride

when Father comes home.
at the time

whenever
when-ev-er
whenever

We will come **whenever** you want us to come.
any time

where
where

"**Where** are you going, Tom?" said Bob.
"To what place

I will go with you **wherever** you go. any place	**wherever** where-ev-er *wherever*
Bob doesn't know **whether** he can go or not. **Whether** it rains or snows, we must go to school.	**whether** wheth-er *whether*
I want this apple. **Which** one do you want?	**which** *which*
I will read **while** you write. at the time	**while** *while*
Bob would not let his dog into the house. The dog started to **whine.** cry softly. (whines whined whining)	**whine** *whine*
Grandfather is good to his horses. He does not **whip** them. hit I like **whipped** cream on jello. **Whipped** cream is white and fluffy. (whips whipped whipping)	**whip** *whip*
This man has **whiskers.** **Whiskers** are hairs that grow on a man's face. Our cat has **whiskers.** (whisker)	**whiskers** whis-kers *whiskers*

A B C D E F G H I J K L M N O P Q R S T U V Ⓦ X Y Z

whisper
whis-per
whisper

Baby likes to whisper in Mother's ear.
speak in a low voice

I like to talk out loud.
(whispers   whispered   whispering)

whistle
whis-tle
whistle

This is a **whistle.**

The **whistle** makes a noise
when you blow through it.

Bob can **whistle** through his lips.
(whistles   whistled   whistling)

white
white

Coal is black.

The snowman is **white.**

who
who

There was an old woman
Who lived in a shoe.

Who is ringing the doorbell?

whole
whole

This is a whole apple.
all of an

This is not a whole apple.
part of an

whooping cough
whoop-ing cough
whooping cough

Tom could not go to school.

He had **whooping cough.**

He coughs very hard.

The other children might get **it**
if he went to school.

The black hat is mine. **Whose** hat is this one? To whom does this one belong?	**whose** *whose*
Jack did not come to school Monday. The teacher asked, " **Why** did you not come, Jack?" "What is the reason you did	**why** *why*
Wicked people do bad things. It is **wicked** to steal.	**wicked** wick-ed *wicked*
The window is **wide.** not narrow. (wider widest)	**wide** *wide*
The farmer makes the garden. The farmer's **wife** washes the dishes. Father is the husband. Mother is the **wife.** (wives)	**wife** *wife*
This is a **wig** of long, curly hair. Mary is going to wear it in the play. (wigs)	**wig** *wig*
This is the Indian's **wigwam.** tent. The Indian lives in a **wigwam.** (wigwams)	**wigwam** wig-wam *wigwam*

A B C D E F G H I J K L M N O P Q R S T U V W X Y Z

wild
wild

The dog is a tame animal.

The lion is a **wild** animal.
not a tame

(wilder   wildest)

---

will
will

He **will** be ready when you come.
He **will** see you after school.

---

willing
will-ing
willing

The boy was **willing** to work.
ready and wanted

---

win
win

The boys are running a race
to the fence.

Who will **win** the race?
get to the fence first?

(wins   winning   won)

---

wind
wind

The **wind** is blowing the flag.
I closed the window to keep out
the cold **wind.**

(winds   windy)

---

wind
wind

See Grandma **wind** the yarn into a ball.
turn

I **wind** my watch every morning.

(winds   winding   wound)

This is a **windmill** you would see in Holland.

The farmer has a **windmill** to pump water for his horses.

The wind makes the **windmill** pump the water.

(windmills)

windmill
wind-mill
windmill

The **window** is broken.

(windows)

window
win-dow
window

The flower stands on the

window sill.
bottom of the window.

(window sills)

window sill
win-dow sill
window sill

The bird has two **wings.**

He flies with his **wings.**

(wing)

The airplane has two **wings.**

wings
wings

In summer it is warm.

In **winter** it is cold.

It snows in **winter.**

(winters)

winter
win-ter
winter

A
B
C
D
E
F
G
H
I
J
K
L
M
N
O
P
Q
R
S
T
U
V
Ⓦ
X
Y
Z

wipe
wipe

See the boy **wipe** his face dry with a towel.

(wipes   wiped   wiping)

wire
wire

This is a **wire** fence.

The telephone **wires** are fastened to the poles.

(wires)

wise
wise

The man is very | **wise.**
| smart.

(wiser   wisest)

wish
wish

The fairy told the old man

to | make a **wish.**
| ask for what he wanted most.

I | **wish** you | a Merry Christmas.
| hope you have |

(wishes   wished   wishing)

witch
witch

This is the **witch** the fairy told us about.

(witches)

with
with

This is a boy | **with** | his cat.
| by the side of |

We live **with** our father and mother.

Father will be there **within** the next hour. sometime in	**within** with-in *within*
This is a pan **without** handles. with no	**without** with-out *without*
Baby was asleep. She **woke** up when the bell rang. (wake wakes waking)	**woke** *woke*
The **wolf** looks something like a dog. He met Little Red Riding Hood in the woods. (wolves)	**wolf** *wolf*
The **woman** is sitting. The man is standing. (women)	**woman** wom-an *woman*
Here are two **women**. (woman)	**women** wom-en *women*
The boys ran a race to the fence. Bob **won** the race. got to the fence first. (win wins winning)	**won** *won*
I **won't** be here long. will not	**won't** *won't*

A B C D E F G H I J K L M N O P Q R S T U V **W** X Y Z

wood
wood

Furniture is made of **wood.**

Some houses are made of **wood.**

This is the **woods**
where trees and flowers grow.

(woods)

woodcutter
wood-cut-ter
woodcutter

A **woodcutter** cuts down trees.

(woodcutters)

wooden
wood-en
wooden

Baby plays with a **wooden** doll.
doll made of wood.

woodman
wood-man
woodman

A **woodman,** or woodsman,
lives and works
in the woods.

(woodmen)

woodpecker
wood-peck-er
woodpecker

This **woodpecker** has a red head.

His tail helps him in climbing.

His bill is strong.

He picks through the bark of the tree
to get bugs to eat.

(woodpeckers)

wool
wool

We get **wool** from sheep.
short, soft hair

Sheep's **wool** is made into yarn and cloth.

(woolen   woolly)

	word
dog ran shop cat These are **words**. Baby can say the **word** cat. (words)	*word*
I put on my blue dress yesterday. I **wore** it all day. (wear wears wearing worn)	**wore** *wore*
I like to **work** in my garden. (works worked working)	**work** *work*
This is Father's **workbench**. He keeps his tools on the **workbench**. (workbenches)	**workbench** work-bench *workbench*
This is a picture of the **world**. / earth. (worlds)	**world** *world*
This is a **worm**. Birds eat **worms**. (worms)	**worm** *worm*

A
B
C
D
E
F
G
H
I
J
K
L
M
N
O
P
Q
R
S
T
U
V
Ⓦ
X
Y
Z

A
B
C
D
E
F
G
H
I
J
K
L
M
N
O
P
Q
R
S
T
U
V
(W)
X
Y
Z

worn *worn*	Mary likes to wear her pink dress. She has **worn** it two times. (wear wears wore wearing)
worse *worse*	Bill is sick. He is **worse** today. not so well I write **worse** than Bob does. more poorly
worst *worst*	Jim is a bad boy, but Henry is the **worst** boy in school.
worth *worth*	Will you sell me your marbles? How much money are they **worth?**
would *would*	I am going to school. **Would** you like to go, too?
wouldn't *wouldn't*	Jack **wouldn't** drink milk. would not

wound *wound*	Grandma **wound** the yarn
	    into a ball.
	
	    Grandpa **wound** the clock
	      so it would run.
	(wind winds winding)

wrap *wrap*	Mother will **wrap up** my lunch for me. put a paper around (wraps wrapped wrapping)

Mary has a **wreath** of flowers on her head. (wreaths)	**wreath** *wreath*
The **wren** is a very small bird. The **wren** has a sweet song. **Wrens** build nests in bushes or birdhouses that children build for them. (wrens)	**wren** *wren*
This tool is a **wrench**. Father uses a **wrench** when he fixes a tap in the sink. (wrenches)	**wrench** *wrench*
A **wristwatch** is worn on the wrist of the hand. It tells the time, just as a clock does. (wrist-watches)	**wristwatch** wrist-watch *wristwatch*
See Mary **write** on the blackboard. She **writes** with her right hand. (writes wrote writing written)	**write** *write*
Mary spelled three words right and two **wrong.** not right.	**wrong** *wrong*
Mary **wrote** her name on the blackboard. (write writes writing written)	**wrote** *wrote*

A B C D E F G H I J K L M N O P Q R S T U V W X Y Z

A
B
C
D
E
F
G
H
I
J
K
L
M
N
O
P
Q
R
S
T
U
V
W
(X)
Y
Z

Xmas *Xmas*	**Xmas** is a way to write Christmas.
x-rays *x-rays*	The doctor can take a picture of your bones with **x-rays.**
xylophone xy-lo-phone *xylophone*	This is a **xylophone.** It makes sweet music. You play on a **xylophone** with hammers. (xylophones)

yard
yard

The children do not play in the street.

They play in the | **yard.**
place around the house. |

Mother bought a **yard** of ribbon.

A **yard** is 36 inches or 3 feet.

(yards)

---

yarn
yarn

Sweaters are made of **yarn.**

Mother made Baby's bonnet of **yarn.**

Yarn is like a heavy thread.

Woolen **yarn** is warm.

SILVER YARN SUPER

---

yawn
yawn

When Baby is sleepy

she | **yawns.**
opens her mouth wide. |

When I am sleepy I **yawn,** too.

(yawns   yawning   yawned)

---

year
year

How old are you?

"I am six **years** old," said Betty.

There are four seasons in each **year.**

(years)

---

yell
yell

The boys | **yell** | when their team wins.
cry out |

(yells   yelled   yelling)

A
B
C
D
E
F
G
H
I
J
K
L
M
N
O
P
Q
R
S
T
U
V
W
X
Ⓨ
Z

yellow yel-low *yellow*	Dandelions are **yellow.** Butter is **yellow.** Lemons are **yellow.** (yellowish)
yes *yes*	I wanted to go. Mother said, **"Yes,** you may go."
yesterday yes-ter-day *yesterday*	Today is Monday. **Yesterday** was Sunday. The day before today
yet *yet*	Father has not come home **yet.** up to now.
yolk *yolk*	The yellow part of the egg is the **yolk.** (yolks)
you *you*	Mother was going for a ride. "I want to go with **you,"** said Fred. The pencil does not belong to me. It belongs to **you.**
young *young*	This is a **young** man. He is 18 years old. This is an old man. He is 80 years old. (younger youngest)

This is my ball. Is that **your** ball? 　　(yours)	**your** *your*
You're a big boy now. You are	**you're** *you're*
Is this ball **yours**? Does this ball belong to you? 　　(your)	**yours** *yours*
I do not like to play by myself. Do you like to play by **yourself**? 　　(yourselves)	**yourself** your-self *yourself*

A B C D E F G H I J K L M N O P Q R S T U V W X Y Z

zebra
ze-bra
zebra

This animal is **a zebra.**

I saw him at the zoo.

He has dark stripes.

(zebras)

---

zero
ze-ro
zero

It is very cold today.

It is 5 below **zero.**
0.

Bob missed all the words.

The teacher put **a zero** on **his** paper.

A zero means "nothing."

(zeros)

---

zinnias
zin-ni-as
zinnias

These flowers are **zinnias.**

They are of many colors.

Zinnias last a long time.

(zinnia)

---

zone
zone

When you cross a wide street, stand in the

safety **zone.**
place marked off for people to stand in.

(zones)

---

zoo
zoo

We saw all kinds of animals at the **zoo.**

(zoos)

THINGS YOU WILL WANT TO KNOW

Days of the Week

Sunday—Sun.
Monday—Mon.
Tuesday—Tues.
Wednesday—Wed.
Thursday—Thurs.
Friday—Fri.
Saturday—Sat.

Months of the Year

January—Jan.
February—Feb.
March—Mar.
April—Apr.
May
June
July
August—Aug.
September—Sept.
October—Oct.
November—Nov.
December—Dec.

Special Days

New Year's Day—Jan. 1
Lincoln's Birthday—Feb. 12
Valentine's Day—Feb. 14
Washington's Birthday—Feb. 22
Easter Sunday
Memorial Day—May 30
Flag Day—June 14
Fourth of July—July 4
Labor Day—First Monday
   in September
Columbus Day—October 12
Election Day—First Tuesday after
   First Monday in November
Veterans Day—November 11
(In Canada, it is Remembrance Day.)
Thanksgiving Day—4th Thursday
   in November
Christmas Day—December 25

Measures

12 inches make 1 foot
3 feet make one yard
5,280 feet make one mile

2 pints make 1 quart
4 quarts make 1 gallon

Weights

16 ounces make 1 pound
2,000 pounds make 1 ton